TRACING
YOUR
FAMILY H

ROYAL AIR FORCE

compiled by Angela Wootton,
edited by Sarah Paterson

IMPERIAL WAR MUSEUM

IMPERIAL WAR MUSEUM

ISBN 1 904 89725 8
2nd Edition

CONTENTS

PREFACE

Day in, day out – and for many years past – rather more than a third of all the public enquiries received by the Museum's Department of Printed Books staff have concerned family history. In many cases we answer these using our knowledge of military history and military institutions and with information from our own rich collections. However, we can also provide accurate referral to the many sources and contacts we know, both elsewhere in the Museum and at scores of other specialist institutions and resources far and wide. The details change over time and new sources emerge. We have to keep up to date with these developments if we are to maintain the quality of our service. With the *Tracing Your Family History* series we aim to share our knowledge with you, helping you to find and understand the information that is available. This second edition of *Tracing Your Family History: Royal Air Force* does just that. It has been comprehensively revised with all the latest information that we ourselves use in our enquiry work.

We are grateful for all the advice and help we have received from Museum colleagues and from other organisations in the preparation of this guide and its predecessor.

Richard Golland
Keeper
Department of Printed Books

ABOUT THE MUSEUM

One of the founding principles behind the establishment of the Imperial War Museum (IWM) in 1917, was its function as a collective memory. Although the original plan for listing the names of the fallen as an intrinsic part of the building never materialised, the Museum has always regarded the individual and his or her experience as being of paramount importance. In his opening address in June 1920, Sir Alfred Mond 'the father of the Imperial War Museum' declared the hope that the collection would be made *'so complete that every individual, man or woman, sailor, soldier, airman or civilian who contributed, however obscurely, to the final result, may be able to find in these galleries an example or illustration of the sacrifice he made or the work he did, and in the archives some record of it.'* Consequently, today we can offer a wealth of material to the family history researcher.

A walk around the main displays on the major conflicts of the century at the Museum in Lambeth Road can help provide a context for a relative's service. There are also additional branches at Duxford in Cambridgeshire, HMS *Belfast*, moored on the Thames opposite the Tower of London, the Churchill Museum and Cabinet War Rooms off Whitehall and Imperial War Museum North in Manchester.

The scope of the Museum encompasses all twentieth century conflict, concentrating on the British and Commonwealth involvement since 1914. In an age of total war, every family in the United Kingdom has been affected in some way. The study of family history, perhaps boosted by the greater availability of information on the internet, has grown considerably over recent years. From schoolchildren interviewing grandparents to local historians writing commemorative histories, the burgeoning growth of this popular activity has made it a real industry. Many of the individuals engaged in research can learn much from the material housed at the Imperial War Museum – original art works and objects of war, personal letters and diaries, contemporary film and photographs, retrospective recorded interviews, and the invaluable collection of printed materials, journals, maps and ephemera. Research may be done in any of the reference departments of the Museum – the Departments of Art, Documents, Exhibits and Firearms, Film and Photograph Archives, Printed Books and the Sound Archive. Access to these collections is both welcomed and encouraged, although a prior appointment is usually necessary. Initial approaches can be made by telephone, letter or e-mail, and staff can provide advice about how to proceed with an enquiry and what materials might be available.

For the family researcher, the first port of call will generally be the Department of Printed Books. This constitutes a national reference library containing well over 150,000 books and pamphlets, 30,000 journals and an impressive range of individual maps and ephemera items, such as ration-books, propaganda leaflets and song-sheets. It is important to stress that the Imperial War Museum **does not** hold any personal service records or official documentation, although through both this booklet and our normal enquiry service, we can offer advice on what and where remaining sources may still be found. We **do** have a wide range of items in our collections which will assist the researcher. These can all be consulted under one roof, with experienced staff on-hand to direct and answer enquiries.

The primary aim of this booklet is to help the enquirer find out about individuals who served in the Royal Air Force. Some basic information is given in the following paragraphs, and useful book titles which will help those unfamiliar with the subject, are given in the bibliography at the end. All of these titles are held by the Museum and can be consulted in the Reading Room, but for those unable to make a personal visit, full publication details are given to enable other copies of the books to be ordered through the public library system. Addresses of the various institutions which may assist can also be found listed in Appendix III.

Strenuous efforts have been made to ensure that the information contained in this booklet is accurate. If any errors have inadvertently been made, we would appreciate it if these could be drawn to our attention so that amendments can appear in later editions.

ORGANISATION OF THE ROYAL AIR FORCE

British military aviation owes its origin to the Corps of Royal Engineers Air Battalion which was established in 1911. In 1912 the Air Battalion was absorbed into the Royal Flying Corps (RFC) which also functioned as part of the Army. The RFC was divided into a Military Wing and a Naval Wing (which became the Royal Naval Air Service (RNAS) in July 1914). In the course of the three years after the outbreak of war in 1914 the RFC underwent a vast expansion in personnel, equipment and operations. It is important to remember that many men transferred to the RFC from other Army regiments or corps rather than joining the RFC directly. On 1 April 1918 the RFC and the RNAS were combined to form the Royal Air Force (RAF). By November 1918 the RAF had reached a total strength of over 390,000 officers and men and had over 22,500 aeroplanes.

After the First World War the size of the RAF was reduced drastically. Although the Auxiliary Air Force (AAF) was formed in 1924, major expansion did not begin until 1934/35. In 1936 the Royal Air Force Volunteer Reserve (RAFVR) was formed. The development programme was given further impetus by the Munich crisis in September 1938. At the start of the Second World War in September 1939 the RAF Reserve (former RAF personnel) and the RAFVR were called to permanent service and the AAF was embodied into the RAF. Under war conditions the RAF once again expanded. By July 1944, it had reached the highest personnel strength in its history with a total of just over 1,185,000 officers and other ranks (including a total of over 170,000 officers and other ranks in the Women's Auxiliary Air Force).

After the end of the war in August 1945 organisational changes and fluctuations in strength would occur in response to the Cold War and the withdrawal from the Empire.

ROYAL AUXILIARY AIR FORCE

The first four squadrons of the Auxiliary Air Force (AAF) were set up in 1925. Their members were volunteers who were recruited on a local basis and who trained in the evenings, and at weekends, and attended a fortnight's summer camp of intensive training with the regular (full-time) RAF. Like the county regiments of the Army the AAF squadrons had local links with particular cities or areas and by September 1939 there were about twenty of these flying squadrons. At the beginning of the war recruitment to the AAF was ended so that there would only be a single channel of entry to the RAF, although the AAF squadrons retained their identity throughout the war years. In December 1947, King George VI awarded the AAF the prefix 'Royal' (always known as the RAuxAF to avoid confusion with the Royal Australian Air Force). The introduction of jet aircraft and more technically advanced ground equipment meant that, on cost grounds, the maintenance of the RAuxAF squadrons became increasingly difficult to justify and all the flying squadrons were disbanded by the middle of 1957. Since then RAuxAF units of various kinds have continued to operate, but none have been equipped with aircraft. In 1997 the RAuxAF absorbed the RAFVR, with the exception of its training element which still continues as the RAFVR(T). The present day RAuxAF provides support to the RAF in various roles, including airfield defence, air movements, aero-medical evacuation, intelligence and public relations.

ROYAL AIR FORCE VOLUNTEER RESERVE

The Royal Air Force Volunteer Reserve was created as part of the RAF's expansion in the mid 1930s and entry began in April 1937. The RAFVR was intended to be a reserve for the whole Air Force and did not have separate units of its own as the Auxiliary Air Force did. The original purpose of the RAFVR was to teach young men with no previous service experience to fly in their spare time. Later, sections were formed for other categories of airmen. All entrants had the rank of airman and the possibility of promotion to commissioned rank only came at a later stage. With the coming of the Second World War all 'hostilities only' enlistments became members of the RAFVR and during the war it was the largest element of the RAF. From 1945 onwards it continued to exist, but in a much reduced capacity. Unlike the RAuxAF which was organised as units, personnel of the RAFVR were appointed on an individual basis, and sent where they were needed. In 1997 the RAFVR was absorbed into the Royal Auxiliary Air Force.

RAF ORGANISATIONAL STRUCTURE

COMMANDS

The highest formation, under the central control of the War Office (to 1918), Air Ministry (1918-1964) or Ministry of Defence (1964 onwards), is the Command, from which all other branches of the 'chain of command' descend. There have been significant organisational differences between home and overseas commands. In the latter, particularly in wartime, the chain of command was not straightforward. Some RAF units would report via a regional Command structure, while other units might report directly to headquarters in the United Kingdom. For further information see the chapters on 'RAF Structure' and 'The Overseas Commands' in *The Source Book of the RAF* by Ken Delve (Airlife, Shrewsbury, Shropshire, 1994).

GROUPS

One or more Groups are subordinate to a Command and obey its instructions. Groups could be composed of bomber or fighter squadrons. There have also been, at different times, coastal, maintenance, training and other kinds of groups. Groups formed overseas tended to have a more general operational function and to comprise more than one type of squadron/unit. In Britain during the Second World War, Bomber Command's Groups were organised on a geographical basis. This was also true of Fighter Command's Groups in the earlier years of the war. (Many of the books dealing with Fighter Command in the Battle of Britain and with Bomber Command's operations during the Second World War provide illustrations of how the process of passing down orders from command to groups to squadrons worked in practice – see Appendix IV). In the course of the history of the RAF the nature of groups has varied a great deal.

WINGS

A Wing was an organisation designed to bring together units under a single commander at a more local level, with the units usually having the same or complementary functions. Wings tended to have a short term operational function, such as the Wings in the 2nd Tactical Air Force in north-west Europe in 1944-1945. Wings could be both flying and ground units.

SQUADRONS

The term Squadron can denote both flying and ground units. A (flying) squadron in the Royal Air Force is the bearer of tradition in the same way as a regiment in the Army or a ship in the Royal Navy. It is a fighting unit, similar to a naval vessel or a battalion of an infantry regiment. Squadrons are generally smaller than Wings and larger than Flights. The distinguishing feature of most flying squadrons is that they have an independent identity. This is signified by the squadron's individual number which is allocated from a series centrally controlled at Ministry level.

The actual establishment of men and aircraft in a squadron has varied for practical reasons. In the late 1930s the standard number of aircraft was about 12 but during the Second World War the numbers of aircraft on a squadron frequently rose to over 20. Most (flying) squadrons in the RAF have been identified by one, two or three digits, 695 being the highest number which has been used. If a squadron has a number of 900 or higher, or a four-figure number (other than the example given in the section on 'Flights' below), it is likely that it is, or was, a unit of the RAF Regiment, a balloon unit or some other unit of this kind.

A system of using 'blocks' of numbers for squadrons evolved in the 1930s and developed during the Second World War, when expansion and the incorporation of Commonwealth and Allied units brought about the need for further number 'blocks'. Not all numbers within a particular block were necessarily used, nor did all squadrons exist at the same time. The following is a brief simplified guide to the number 'blocks':

1-99	**RFC/RAF**
200-299	**ex RNAS**
300-309	**Polish**
310-313	**Czechoslovak**
315-318	**Polish**
320-322	**Dutch**
326-329	**Free French**
330-334	**Norwegian**
335-336	**Greek**
340-347	**Free French**
349-350	**Belgian**
351-352	**Yugoslav**
353-399	**RAF** (only eight of this block of numbers were ever used)
400-443	**Royal Canadian Air Force**
450-467	**Royal Australian Air Force**
485-490	**Royal New Zealand Air Force**
500-504	**Auxiliary Air Force**
510-598	**RAF** (only about fifty of this block of numbers were ever used)
600-616	**Auxiliary Air Force**
617-644	**RAF**
650-673	**Army-associated allocation.** Air Observation Post squadrons and others. Since September 1957 this block of numbers has been dedicated to Army Air Corps units.
674-699	**RAF allocation** (only eight of this block of numbers were ever used)
700-799	**Fleet Air Arm catapult units originally; later second-line Naval squadrons**
800-899	**Fleet Air Arm carrier- and land-based operational squadrons**
900-999	**Barrage balloon squadrons**

FLIGHTS

Flights are smaller than squadrons and can be of two types. Squadrons have often been divided into three or four flights and in war situations flights were sometimes detached from their 'parent' squadron and sent to another airfield for some specific operational purpose. The other type of flight are individual units which have been formed and numbered for particular roles but have not been large enough to qualify for squadron status. The one exception was 1435 Flight which was formed in Malta in 1941 and in August 1942 was redesignated 1435 Squadron.

RANKS

Before 1 April 1918 these were the same as Army ranks. When the RAF was established new ranks were introduced, although these did not come into effect immediately. Every RAF rank has its equivalent in the Army and the Royal Navy, and it should be noted that the 'steps' in rank remain the same. The rank structure of non-commissioned officers' and airmens' ranks has varied at times whereas officers' ranks have remained more or less constant from the First World War era to the present day.

In the context of the RAF it should be emphasised that the rank name does not indicate whether or not an individual was employed on flying duties. Throughout its history the RAF has had many members who may rarely or never have flown in an aircraft. This was particularly the case in the later years of the Second World War, when the RAF had the highest number of personnel in its history. Great effort went into making sure that the aircraft were in a fit state to be flown, and that the men flying them were trained, clothed, catered for and paid. Many more members of the RAF were involved in administration and maintenance than involved directly with flying. All those officers listed under the General Duties Branch in the *Air Force List* can be assumed to have held a flying brevet (ie were qualified as pilots or aircrew).

Comparative table of officer ranks (in descending order)

Royal Air Force	Army	Royal Navy
Marshal of the Royal Air Force	Field Marshal	Admiral of the Fleet
Air Chief Marshal	General	Admiral
Air Marshal	Lieutenant General	Vice Admiral
Air Vice Marshal	Major General	Rear Admiral
Air Commodore	Brigadier	Commodore
Group Captain	Colonel	Captain
Wing Commander	Lieutenant Colonel	Commander
Squadron Leader	Major	Lieutenant-Commander
Flight Lieutenant	Captain	Lieutenant
Flying Officer	Lieutenant	Sub-Lieutenant
Pilot Officer	Second-Lieutenant	Midshipman (junior to Army and RAF ranks)

RAF non-commissioned ranks (in descending order)

RFC	RAF (1918)
Warrant Officer	Sergeant Major I or Chief Master Mechanic
Quartermaster-Sergeant	Sergeant Major II or Master Mechanic

Flight Sergeant	Flight Sergeant or Chief Mechanic
Sergeant	Sergeant or Sergeant Mechanic
Corporal	Corporal or Corporal Mechanic
Air Mechanic I	Air Mechanic 1st Class
Air Mechanic II	Private 1st Class or Air Mechanic 2nd Class
Air Mechanic III	Private 2nd Class or Air Mechanic 3rd Class

RAF (1919-1951)	**RAF (1951-1964)**
Sergeant Major 1st Class	Warrant Officer or Master Technician
Sergeant Major 2nd Class	Flight Sergeant
Flight Sergeant	Chief Technician
Sergeant	Sergeant or Senior Technician
Corporal	Corporal or Corporal Technician
-	Junior Technician
-	Senior Aircraftman
Leading Aircraftman	Leading Aircraftman
Aircraftman 1st Class	Aircraftman 1st Class
Aircraftman 2nd Class	Aircraftman 2nd Class

The rank structure for the RAF in 1918 also included the title of Clerk for all the ranks in the table ranging from Chief Master Clerk down to Clerk 3rd Class. In 1933 the rank of Sergeant Major was abolished and replaced by the single rank of Warrant Officer. In 1964 Master Technician was replaced with Master Aircrew, Senior Technician and Corporal Technician were no longer used, and Aircraftman 1st and 2nd Class was replaced by Aircraftman.

ROYAL NAVAL AIR SERVICE AND FLEET AIR ARM

The history of the organisational relationship between the Royal Naval Air Service, the Fleet Air Arm and the Royal Air Force is very complex. Although information can be found in some of the titles listed in the bibliography, we can supply details of other useful publications if required.

The RNAS was set up as the RFC's naval wing. In July 1914 the Admiralty took over the control of the Naval Wing from the War Office and it became known as the Royal Naval Air Service (RNAS). Both the RFC and the RNAS had important roles in operations in the course of the First World War but nevertheless the split between the RFC and the RNAS led to confusion, inefficiency and ill feeling. When the RAF was established the military and naval wings were merged and RNAS squadrons were given new squadron numbers.

In the inter-war era there was an ongoing dispute between the RAF and the Royal Navy regarding the control of naval aviation. Financial constraints and inter-service rivalry were also factors in this controversy. The problem was studied by a series of government committees. Although an improved working relationship was achieved by the end of the 1920s, the dispute was not really resolved until 1937 when the Royal Navy once again took control of the new 'Naval Air Branch'. This arrangement has continued to the present day, although the designation of Fleet Air Arm only came into use officially in 1953.

WOMEN'S SERVICES

In February 1917, the Women's Army Auxiliary Corps was formed to accept women for military duties in non-combat areas in France and (later) in Britain. In February 1918, the Women's Royal Naval Service was set up along similar lines. Additionally, the Women's Legion, a private organisation, provided a 'corps' of drivers for cars and other vehicles in military formations. All three services were involved in duties which were linked to the Royal Flying Corps and the Royal Naval Air Service. It was therefore decided to form a separate women's service and the Women's Royal Air Force (WRAF) came into existence on 1 April 1918. By the time of the Armistice in November 1918 there were 25,000 women in the WRAF. The WRAF was disbanded as an economy measure in 1920.

In May 1939, the Air Council decided to form a new women's service for the RAF and in the following month the Women's Auxiliary Air Force (WAAF) was set up. The new force was intended not only to release men for operational front-line duty but also to assume a wider and more active role within the service itself, although members of the WAAF were not actively involved in flying aircraft. The WAAF reached its highest strength in April 1943 when it had over 181,000 officers and airwomen in total. After the end of the Second World War the WAAF remained in existence and in 1948 it once again became the Women's Royal Air Force.

In 1994 in line with similar changes in the Army (Women's Royal Army Corps – WRAC) and the Navy (Women's Royal Naval Service – WRNS) the WRAF was abolished and women became fully integrated in the Royal Air Force.

In 1918 it was evident that the new force needed to have its own nursing service and the Royal Air Force Nursing Service was set up in June of that year. After the war, although the WAAF was disbanded, the nursing service remained in existence and in 1923 became Princess Mary's Royal Air Force Nursing Service (PMRAFNS), a name that it has continued to bear to the present day. (Princess Mary, the Princess Royal, was the daughter of King George V). The PMRAFNS continued in existence through the inter-war era, the Second World War and the post-1945 years, and from 1980 has had both female and male personnel.

SERVICE RECORDS

The Imperial War Museum does not hold records of service personnel or official documentation, although the Museum's Department of Printed Books has a large collection of operational histories, unit histories and other, more general, sources of value to the family researcher. Some of these sources are mentioned within the text and also in the list outlined in Appendix IV.

If no details are known about the serviceman or woman, some basic information may be available from the *Absent Voters Lists* of 1918 and the *Service Voters Registers* of 1945, compiled in order to enable servicemen to vote in the constituency of their home address. These should be held by the relevant local library, town hall or county record office. The entries often contain details of address, unit, number and rank. Another good source is the **Family Records Centre, 1 Myddelton Street, London EC1R 1UW** which provides research facilities previously provided at St Catherine's House. Their records include indexes of births, deaths and marriages since 1837, legal adoptions since 1927 and births, deaths and marriages of some British citizens abroad since the late 18th century.

Generally, personnel records for those who served in the Royal Flying Corps and Royal Air Force up to the mid 1920s are now available to the public at **The National Archives, Ruskin Avenue, Kew, Richmond, Surrey TW9 4DU**. If an individual had any service beyond the mid 1920s, records will be held at **RAF Disclosure of Information Office, PMA IM 1B (RAF), Room 5, Building 248A, RAF Personnel**

Management Agency, RAF Innsworth, Gloucester GL3 1EZ.

Records for officers who ceased service before 1 April 1918 will be found under their branch of service. Royal Flying Corps officer records can be located in classes *WO 339* (with indexes in *WO 338*) and *WO 374*. If you can't find the record in either of these classes, try *AIR 76*. Royal Naval Air Service officer records can be found in class *ADM 273* (the **Fleet Air Arm Museum, Centre for Naval Aviation Records and Research, Box D6, RNAS Yeovilton, Yeovil, near Ilchester, Somerset BA22 8HT** also holds copies of similar records).

Records for Royal Air Force officers who ceased service between 1 April 1918 and the end of 1920 are located in class *AIR 76*. It is also worth checking *AIR 1* as these contain additional information.

Men who joined the Royal Flying Corps between 1912 and the outbreak of war in 1914 can be found listed in the publication *A Contemptible Little Flying Corps* by I McInnes and JV Webb (London Stamp Exchange, London, 1991).

Records for other ranks who ceased service before 1 April 1918 are also held according to branch of service. Royal Naval Air Service records for ratings can be found in *ADM 188* (and again some records may be available at the Fleet Air Arm Museum). Many Royal Flying Corps records were destroyed by Second World War bombing and so not all have survived. There are two classes where one might find RFC other ranks – *WO 364* (compiled by the Ministry of

Pensions and consisting of some duplicate information to that contained in the destroyed records – it is unlikely that you will find airmen who died here) and *WO 363*. If your relative's record was amongst those destroyed, you might be able to find some basic information through the First World War Medal Index, which is now available online. Please see the section on **Medal Records** to find out more about this.

Records for most Royal Air Force other ranks who served during the First World War (ie after 1 April 1918) but not during the Second, can be found in The National Archives class *AIR 79* (the records are in service number order and an index to them can be found in *AIR 78*). However, only those whose service number is below 329,000 will be found here (this will not include anyone who enlisted after 1919, and it should be noted that numbers in the *RAF Muster Roll* go up to 409,095 – for more information about this, see the last paragraph in this section and Appendix I). This does mean that the records of some RAF servicemen who saw service in the First World War will still be at RAF Innsworth.

You can visit The National Archives in person to do your own research (remember to take some documentary means of identification in order to obtain a reader's ticket). If a visit is not possible The National Archives offer a paid research service or can provide a list of 'approved' professional researchers. However, for anyone intending to do their own genealogical research, The National Archives has produced invaluable guides to their holdings in the form of published handbooks and Records Information Sheets and leaflets, a number of which are now accessible via their website at **www.nationalarchives.gov.uk** under 'Research, education and online exhibitions'. Two handbooks which are particularly relevant are *Tracing your Ancestors in the Public Record Office*, 6th revised edition edited by Amanda Bevan (Richmond, Surrey, Public Record Office, 2002) and *Air Force Records for Family Historians* by William Spencer (Richmond, Surrey, Public Record Office, 2000).

Enquiries concerning RAF personnel records from the mid 1920s up to the present day should be directed to the **RAF Disclosure of Information Office, PMA IM 1B (RAF), Room 5, Building 248A, RAF Personnel Management Agency, RAF Innsworth, Gloucester GL3 1EZ**. A search fee of £30.00 will be levied. Information will be released to the service personnel concerned or their next of kin. Genealogical enquiries to any branch of the Ministry of Defence should be made in writing, and do not receive priority as their principal concern is to respond to official enquiries relating to welfare, employment, pensions and legal matters.

All RAF officers are listed by name in the *Air Force List*. This was first published in 1918 and the Department of Printed Books has a near complete set up to the present day. A virtually complete set of the *Army List* from 1914 onward is also held, through which the ranks and dates of promotion of RFC/RAF officers can be traced up to March 1918. From April 1918, details will appear in the *Air Force List*. Those serving in the Royal Naval Air Service can be traced in the same way using the *Navy List*. You do need to be certain of the full name of the individual you want to research as there can be several people listed with the same surname and similar initials. During both world wars the volumes became very large (in the First World War the *Army List* was published monthly). Names appear in the indexes at the back of each volume, from where one is referred to the appropriate column in the volume. The lists are organised by branch of service (eg General Duties, Medical, Stores, Accounts), and then by rank and seniority. It can generally be assumed that those officers whose names appear under the General Duties branch held a flying brevet (ie were qualified as pilots or aircrew).

From 1918 to 1945 the *Air Force List* was published monthly. Later it appeared at less frequent intervals and today it is an annual publication. It should be noted that the entries for the RFC in the *Army List* do not include details of squadrons, nor are such details included in the 1918-1919 *Air Force Lists*. The *Lists* published between 1920 and 1938 showed units and dates of postings, allowing you to trace an officer's movements. From 1938 onwards, for security and administrative reasons, these details were no longer included and they have never been re-introduced. Thus, for the periods of both world wars and post-1945, the lists are less informative than might be expected.

There are no equivalent lists for other ranks but the Department of Printed Books does hold a copy of the *RAF Muster Roll* of April 1918, which gives very brief details of NCOs and airmen. The names appear in the order of their service numbers and there is no index. The *Muster Roll* can sometimes be useful to confirm information which is already known but it is difficult to use unless you already have an airman's service number. The details given for each man include his RNAS or RFC trade classification, the Air Force trade classification to which he was re-mustered, his RNAS rank or RFC rank/appointment, his new rank in the Air Force, his date of joining or last promotion, his normal rate of pay and his term of enlistment. The great majority enlisted for the Duration of the War (DW) while a minority had an Open Enlistment (OE).

MEDAL RECORDS

Campaign medals are given to airmen who are eligible for them because they served in a particular theatre of war between given dates. Details about these medals can be found in the books in the reading list. Some technical terms that might prove helpful when reading through this section include definitions for 'clasp' and 'bar'. Both refer to a narrow metal strip worn on the medal ribbon, but a bar denotes a second award for gallant or distinguished service (and a bar can be given for each subsequent award). The term bar should, therefore, only be used in connection with gallantry medals. The term clasp is used in the context of campaign medals (where it will usually include some description eg.'5th Aug-22nd Nov 1914','Burma' or 'Palestine 1945-1948'). The word clasp is also used to denote second or subsequent awards of Long Service and Good Conduct Medals or Territorial decorations. The term 'obverse' refers to the front of the medal or the side bearing the principal design, while the 'reverse' is the subordinate side of the medal.

FIRST WORLD WAR

The First World War campaign medals are described in detail on the Imperial War Museum website (**http://collections.iwm.org.uk/server/show/ConWebDoc.986**), but a brief description of the 1914 and 1914-15 Star, British War Medal and Victory Medal can be found in the following paragraphs. First World War medals are useful for the family historian because they usually include the name and some unit details of the man they were issued to (engraved on the back of the 1914 and 1914-15 Stars and around the rim of the British War Medal and Victory Medal). A useful book for deciphering the initials on medals and for general advice is *Collecting and Researching the Campaign Medals of the Great War* by HJ Williamson.

The National Archives holds the First World War Medal Roll (*WO 329*), and this can be accessed by using the Medal Index Cards (*WO 372*). This provides an alphabetical list of those who qualified for the 1914 Star, 1914-15 Star, British War Medal, Victory Medal, Territorial Force War Medal and/or the Silver War Badge. This should provide some basic details of a airman's service even if his service record was destroyed. The index cards can now be viewed online at **http://www.nationalarchives.gov.uk/documentsonline/** You can search the index for free, and this will provide you with the name, corps or regiment, regimental number and rank. When you have the right man (or have narrowed your search to a few likely candidates) you can order a digitised image of the medal index card for £3.50 (correct price at time of going to press).

If a campaign medal record can be found this should provide some basic details of an airman's service even if his service record was destroyed. Full details of how to use the Medal Roll can be found in the publication *Army Service Records of the First World War* by William Spencer and on The National Archives website.

The **1914 Star** (often known as the 'Mons Star') is a bronze crowned four-pointed star with two crossed swords and a wreath of oak leaves. A scroll reads '1914' with 'Aug' and 'Nov' above and below this. The ribbon is red, white and blue silk, shaded and watered. It was awarded to those who had served in Belgium or France beween 5 August and midnight on 22 November 1914. A clasp with the inscription '5th Aug-22nd Nov 1914' was issued to those who had served under fire between those dates. The majority of men who received this medal would have been regular soldiers before the outbreak of war (the 'Old Contemptibles') and recipients would always also have received the British War Medal and Victory Medal (the three medals were often known by the nicknames of 'Pip, Squeak and Wilfred' a trio of popular cartoon characters in the *Daily Mail*).

The **1914-15 Star** is very similar to the 1914 Star except that the central scroll has been replaced with '1914-15' and the words 'Aug' and 'Nov' omitted. It was awarded to those who had been on active service in any theatre of war between 4 August 1914 and 31 December 1915 (unless they were already eligible for the 1914 Star).

The **British War Medal** was struck in silver and bronze (the latter issued to non-Europeans serving in units of the Labour Corps). The medal features the coinage head of King George V, with a naked man on horseback on the reverse trampling on the eagle shield of the Central Powers and the symbols of death. The sun, symbolic of victory, rises above, and around the edge are the dates '1914' and '1918'. The silk ribbon has a central vertical stripe of gold with stripes of white and black at each side and borders of royal blue. The medal was awarded to those who had entered a theatre of war on duty or rendered approved service overseas between 5 August 1914 and 11 November 1918. It also covered service in Russia between 1919 and 1920. The British War Medal could be awarded on its own and was often the single medal awarded to men who served in India during the war.

The **Victory Medal** in yellow bronze features the goddess of Victory, Athene Nike, on the obverse and the inscription 'The Great War for civilisation' on the reverse. The silk ribbon is a watered rainbow design with red in the centre. It was awarded to those who served in a theatre of war between 5 August 1914 and 11 November 1918. It was never awarded by itself and when the Victory Medal and British War Medal were issued together they were often known as 'Mutt and Jeff'.

The **Territorial Force War Medal 1914-19** is bronze with the coinage head of King George V on the obverse and has 'Territorial War Medal' around the top. The text 'For Voluntary Service Overseas 1914-19' is enclosed in a wreath. The ribbon is of watered yellow silk with two green vertical stripes. This medal was awarded to members of the Territorial Force who were members on 4 August 1914 or who had previously served four years and rejoined on or before 30 September 1914. They also had to have served outside the United Kingdom between 4 August 1914 and 11 November 1918 and not have been eligible for the 1914 or 1914-1915 Stars.

The **Silver War Badge** is circular and contains the inscription 'For King and Empire' and 'Services Rendered'. It was issued to those who retired or were discharged owing to wounds, ill health or having reached the age of 51. It was first issued in 1916 and continued until 1920.

SECOND WORLD WAR

Second World War campaign medals were not stamped with the holder's name and unit as an economy measure, although arrangements could be made to have this done privately. Eight bronze, six-pointed stars were issued, each with the crowned royal cipher reading 'GRI' with 'VI' below. The title of the medal encircles this with the points of the star protruding behind. A maximum of five stars could be awarded to a single person, and if they qualified for more, a clasp could be attached to the ribbon of the appropriate star (the medal for which they first qualified). The ribbons were personally designed by King George VI and all have symbolic significance.

The **1939-45 Star** has a ribbon which contains equal stripes of dark blue, red and light blue representing the Royal Navy and Merchant Navy, Army and Royal Air Force. It was awarded for six months service between 3 September 1939 and 15 August 1945. RAF personnel qualified for the award for any flying operations against the enemy, provided that two months service had been completed in operational units. Ground crew had to complete six months service in the area of an operational command, with the exception of Dunkirk and Norway. Air crews of fighter aircraft engaged in the Battle of Britain between 10 July and 31 October 1940 were awarded the 'Battle of Britain' clasp.

The **Africa Star** has a buff or sand coloured ribbon with a wide red central stripe bordered by a dark blue and light blue stripe, representing the desert, Army, Royal Navy and Royal Air Force. Three clasps could also be issued: '8th Army', '1st Army' and 'North Africa 1942-43'. The Africa Star was awarded for one or more days' service in North or East Africa between 10 June 1940 and 12 May 1943.

The **Pacific Star** has a ribbon of dark green (representing the jungle) with a central yellow stripe (representing beaches), narrow dark and light blue stripes with wider red stripes at the edges. It was awarded for service in Hong Kong, China and Malaya between 8 December 1941 and 2 September 1945. Service in Burma was excluded, although if an individual was eligible for both stars, a 'Burma' clasp could be worn.

The ribbon of the **Burma Star** has three equal bands of dark blue, red and dark blue. The dark blue bands contain a central stripe of orange, which represents the sun. It was awarded for service in Burma between 11 December 1941 and 2 September 1945. Service in Bengal and Assam was also eligible, as was service in China and Malaya between 16 February 1942 and 2 September 1945. A 'Pacific' clasp was also issued.

The **Italy Star** ribbon contains the Italian national colours of red, white, green, white and red in equal stripes. It was awarded for operational service in Italy and Sicily (also Greece, Corsica, the Aegean, Dodecanese islands, Yugoslavia, Sardinia and Elba) between 11 June 1943 and 8 May 1945.

The **France and Germany Star** has a ribbon of five equal stripes of blue, white, red, white and blue, representing the national colours of the United Kingdom, France and the Netherlands. It was awarded for service, including flying operations, between 6 June 1944 and 8 May 1945 in France, Belgium, the Netherlands and Germany.

The **Air Crew Europe Star** has a pale blue ribbon flanked by a narrow black stripe on each side and black edges, symbolising the continuous day and night flying of the RAF. This star was awarded for operational flying from United Kingdom bases over Europe (including the United Kingdom) for two months between 3 September 1939 and 5 June 1944. Service in operations at sea were not eligible. Two clasps were issued: 'Atlantic' and 'France and Germany'. This is the rarest of the Second World War campaign stars.

The **Atlantic Star** has a shaded and watered blue, white and sea green ribbon. It was awarded for six months service afloat in the Atlantic, home waters, convoys to Russia or certain parts of the south Atlantic. FAA personnel qualified for any operation against the enemy in the specified areas, provided they had two months service in an operational unit and the prior award of the 1939-1945 Star. Army and RAF personnel serving with the Royal or Merchant Navy qualified in the same way as members of the service to which they were attached. Those who were not able to complete the qualifying period and were not eligible for the 1939-1945 Star were awarded the Atlantic Star. Two clasps were issued: 'Air Crew Europe' and 'France and Germany' although only one of these could be issued to any individual.

The **Defence Medal** is made of cupro-nickel with the uncrowned head of King George VI on the obverse and two lions flanking a crowned oak sapling on top of wavy lines (representing the sea) on the reverse. The date '1939' appears at top left and '1945' appears at top right and 'The Defence Medal' appears at the bottom. The ribbon has two wide stripes of green signifying the countryside with two narrow black stripes representing the blackout and a wide central stripe of orange representing fire and bombing. This had a large number of varying conditions relating to eligibility but it was basically awarded for three years' service in the United Kingdom or one year overseas.

The **War Medal 1939-45** is made of cupro-nickel and has the crowned head of King George VI on the obverse. The reverse shows a lion standing on a defeated dragon and has the date '1939' on top of the date '1945'. The ribbon has a narrow red stripe in the centre flanked by two narrow white stripes, thicker dark blue stripes are between the white stripes and the thick red stripes which form the edge of the ribbon. The design represents the Union Flag. The medal was awarded for service of at least twenty-eight days between 3 September 1939 and 2 September 1945.

OTHER CONFLICTS

Specific campaign medals were issued for Korea (1950-1953), the South Atlantic (1982), the Gulf (1990-1991) and Iraq (2003-). The **General Service Medal** (1918-1962) was awarded for service in many different campaigns and would always be given with a clasp, sixteen of which were issued. Some of these include 'S. Persia' (12 November 1918 - 22 June 1919), 'S.E. Asia 1945-46' (awarded to troops serving in the Dutch East Indies and French Indo-China) and Cyprus (1 April 1955 - 18 April 1959). This was succeeded by the **Campaign Service Medal** in 1962. This was awarded to all three services and is often referred to as the General Service Medal. The **Accumulated Campaign Service Medal** was introduced in 1994, for 36 months (not necessarily consecutive) operational service. There was also an **India General Service Medal** covering campaigns between 1908-1935 and 1936-1939 and an **Africa General Service Medal** covering the years 1902-1956. The United Nations also issues campaign medals, usually with different ribbons denoting different peace-keeping operations.

The address to write to for medal enquiries is **Ministry of Defence Medal Office, Building 250, RAF Innsworth, Gloucester GL3 1HW**. It will be necessary to prove that you are next of kin.

LONG SERVICE MEDALS

The **Royal Air Force Long Service and Good Conduct Medal** was instituted in July 1919 and was awarded to other ranks with exemplary service after 18 years (although this was shortened to 15 years in 1977).

The **Royal Air Force Meritorious Service Medal** was instituted in June 1918, originally for meritorious service in the field during the First World War and in Russia (1918-1920). The medal was replaced by the British Empire Medal in 1928, but was revived at the end of 1977 with the same conditions as applied to the Army Meritorious Service Medal (it is awarded to non-commissioned officers with 27 years meritorious service).

GALLANTRY AWARDS

Gallantry medals reward a particular act of bravery but the amount of information available for different decorations does vary considerably. An award can be made more than once and if this happens the recipient will be given a 'bar' to wear on the original medal's ribbon. Notification of an award (which just gives the information that an individual has been awarded a particular decoration) would be published in the *London Gazette* – sometimes the citation (a short description of why the award was given) would accompany this, sometimes this would appear in a later issue and sometimes no citation would appear at all. There was often a considerable delay between the date of the award and the date that the notification, and the citation if appropriate, was published. The practice of publishing citations in the *London Gazette* declined from mid-1916. Again, at the beginning of the Second World War, publication of all citations for gallantry awards was suspended and no citations for Mentions in Despatches are available for any period. Often an individual would be recommended for a particular award, but this would not be granted, or he or she would be awarded a lesser decoration.

The *London Gazette* is a difficult publication to use if you do not already have precise dates/issue details. The National Archives does have a full set of the *London Gazette* together with the all-important indexes. The **Guildhall Library, Aldermanbury, London EC2P 2EJ** also holds a complete set with indexes and acts as the unofficial photocopying service for the *London Gazette* office. It is quite likely that sets of the *London Gazette* will be held by large public reference libraries in various parts of the country.

The *London Gazette* can be accessed online at **www.gazettes-online.co.uk**

Gallantry awards are of two types, immediate and non-immediate. The National Archives will have much of the available documentation about gallantry awards. Awards were frequently noted in squadron operations record books (record class *AIR 27*) or in station operations record books (record classes *AIR 28* and *AIR 29*). Most notifications of awards for gallantry and meritorious service were published in the *London Gazette* but it should be noted that there was always a delay between the receipt of an award and its notification in a *Gazette* issue. Those recommendations for awards which have survived can be found in record class *AIR 2 Code No 30*, but unless the likely date of the recommendation and the theatre of war are known, a search in this record class may be lengthy and complex.

Enquirers are advised to try initially to trace references to gallantry awards in the *London Gazette* or via The National Archives. Written enquiries (from next of kin, with proof of relationship) may be directed to the Ministry of Defence Medal Office at RAF Innsworth (see above).

The **Victoria Cross** is the highest gallantry decoration and is extremely well documented. It can be awarded to all ranks of the three armed services. The Department of Documents at the Imperial War Museum has a collection of Victoria Cross files which can be consulted by appointment. Anybody interested in this award (or in the George Cross which was also awarded to many servicemen) should make an effort to visit the Museum's VC-GC gallery. The Museum's website features the Victoria Cross and the George Cross at these addresses:

Victoria Cross
http://collections.iwm.org.uk/server/show/ConWebDoc.941

George Cross
http://collections.iwm.org.uk/server/show/ConWebDoc.940

The **Distinguished Service Order** was introduced in 1886, and was awarded only to commissioned officers.

In 1918 the RAF instituted four awards for gallantry:

The **Distinguished Flying Cross** was awarded to officers and warrant officers for an act or acts of valour, courage or devotion to duty performed while flying in active operations against the enemy. The ribbon has diagonal narrow purple and white stripes running at an angle from left to right.

The **Distinguished Flying Medal** was awarded to non-commissioned officers and men on the same basis as the Distinguished Flying Cross. It has the same ribbon.

The **Air Force Cross** was awarded to officers and warrant officers for an act or acts of valour, courage or devotion to duty while flying, although not in active operations against the enemy. The ribbon has diagonal narrow crimson and white stripes running at an angle from left to right.

The **Air Force Medal** was awarded to non-commissioned officers and men on the same basis as the Air Force Cross. It was instituted at the same time and has the same ribbon.

The **Conspicuous Gallantry Medal** was originally an award for ratings of the Royal Navy. In 1942 the Conspicuous Gallantry Medal was extended to RAF (and also to Army) other ranks as an award for conspicuous gallantry while flying in active operations against the enemy. The RAF version of this medal, which ranks above the DFM, is known as the **Conspicuous Gallantry Medal (Flying)**. The ribbon is light blue with narrow dark blue marginal stripes. There have only been 110 awards of this rare medal.

In 1993, several radical changes were made to the system of recognising gallantry in the armed forces and under the new arrangements awards were no longer rank-related. The Conspicuous Gallantry Medal, the Conspicuous Gallantry Medal (Flying), the Distinguished Conduct Medal and the Distinguished Service Order were all replaced by the Conspicuous Gallantry Cross, for which all ranks of the armed services are eligible. The Distinguished Service Order is no longer awarded for gallantry but can still be awarded for command and leadership qualities during operations and is open to all ranks. The Distinguished Flying Medal and Air Force Medal were abolished and all ranks became eligible for the Distinguished Flying Cross and Air Force Cross.

Both officers and men can be awarded **Mentions in Despatches**. No medal is issued for this award but a certificate would be received and, in 1920, a multiple-leaved bronze oak leaf emblem was authorised to be worn on the ribbon of the Victory Medal. After 1920 the emblem changed to a single oak leaf and those awarded in the Second World War were worn on the War Medal 1939-1945. Since 1945 those awarded a Mention in Despatches wear the oak leaf emblem on the ribbon of the relevant campaign medal. If the recipient has no campaign medal the emblem can be worn on a piece of grey cloth shaped as a medal ribbon.

The Department of Printed Books holds published sources which might prove helpful, some of which are listed in Appendix IV. It is also possible that you might find details in published squadron histories, autobiographies and biographies and journals. The Department also holds a near complete run of the *London Gazette* from 1914, although without a complete set of the all important indexes.

CASUALTY RECORDS

OFFICIAL RECORDS

The **Commonwealth War Graves Commission, 2 Marlow Road, Maidenhead, Berkshire SL6 7DX** has details of the burial place or commemoration site for all those who died in service between 4 August 1914 and 31 August 1921, and between 3 September 1939 and 31 December 1947. The Commission may charge a search fee for direct enquiries, but their website is freely available to everyone with internet access. The database is called *The Debt of Honour* (and can be consulted at **www.cwgc.org**).

The Department of Printed Books has a complete set of the cemetery and memorial registers published by the CWGC openly available in our Reading Room (although no comprehensive indexes to them are held). Much of the information contained in these can now be found in the *Debt of Honour* database. As well as searching under an individual name, it is also possible to search in the database under the name of a cemetery or memorial. Visiting, location and historical details are given and the 'Cemetery reports' link leads to listings of the Commonwealth war graves in a particular cemetery. In the cases of some larger cemeteries and memorials, plans and photographs are included.

The Commonwealth War Graves Commission may be able to help provide further information about the activities of aircrew if they died of wounds or were killed in action in either of the two world wars. Their records may indicate whether they were pilots, navigators, gunners, etc. Crew from one aircraft would often be buried together if possible.

The principal Air Force memorials for the Second World War are those at Runnymede, Alamein, Singapore, Malta and Ottawa. If an airman died in Britain, on operations or in training, or if his body was recovered on British soil, and his next of kin were in Britain, it was usually the case that the body was returned to the airman's home area for burial. It is unlikely that British airmen will be found buried near to where they were stationed – this did happen in some cases, but it seems to have been the exception rather than the rule. On the other hand, Commonwealth airmen who died in Britain but who did not have next of kin in this country, were often buried near to where they were stationed.

In some countries such as France, Belgium and the Netherlands, single graves of British and Commonwealth airmen may be found in small local cemeteries. Enquirers need to refer to the CWGC or to the database to find grave locations. In Germany, the burials are in a relatively small number of large cemeteries. The remains of airmen and soldiers were concentrated in these cemeteries in the immediate post-war years. In those countries and areas of the world where there are relatively few Commonwealth cemeteries or memorials, tracing a grave location or a memorial inscription can also be fairly straightforward.

Official records of RAF casualties and aircraft losses during the Second World War and from 1945 onwards, are held by the **Ministry of Defence, Air Historical Branch, Building 266, Bentley Priory, Stanmore, Middlesex HA7 3HH**.

These records are not open to the public and enquiries must be made by letter only. Details will only be released to former RAF personnel or to their surviving next of kin.

Enquiries regarding RAF personnel who were killed or died in service and are buried in publicly funded 'non world war' graves (ie outside those periods covered by the Commonwealth War Graves Commission) should be sent by letter only to **Joint Casualty and Compassionate Centre, Armed Forces Personnel Administration Agency, Building 182, RAF Innsworth, Gloucester GL3 1HW**. Please mark your enquiry 'Memorials and Graves'.

PUBLISHED SOURCES

Details of some useful reference works can be found in Appendix IV. For the First World War, various volumes of the *Cross of Sacrifice* series list names in alphabetical order and also provide details of the Commonwealth War Graves Commission's cemetery or memorial in which the individual's name can be found – this can be easily checked in our reading room.

Many local organisations published rolls of service or rolls of honour, and we have a good collection of these, although they were more common for the First World War than for the Second. Schools and colleges often published listings of their old pupils, as did local towns, churches and companies. Information contained in these does vary, but can sometimes be very detailed and may include a photograph.

A frequently requested publication is *The National Roll of the Great War, 1914-1918*. This is unusual in that it lists both those who died and those who survived, as well as those involved in non-military war work, such as female munition workers. However, we believe it to have been compiled on a subscription basis, and as such it is very far from being comprehensive and contains a number of inaccuracies. It also covers only a few geographical areas, such as large cities and towns. The publication was probably begun in 1920, but by 1922 the publishers had already gone into liquidation, having only published fourteen volumes (referred to as sections). The sections published were: 1.London 2.London 3.London 4.Southampton 5.Luton 6.Birmingham 7.London 8.Leeds 9.Bradford 10.Portsmouth 11.Manchester 12.Bedford and Northampton 13.London 14.Salford. The Department of Printed Books has a complete set of these volumes. The Manchester and Salford volumes can be viewed online on the *Spinning the Web: the Story of the Cotton Industry* website at **www.spinningtheweb.org.uk**

Useful listings, local histories or contemporary newspapers may be located in the home area of the individual one is researching. Local studies libraries and county record offices should be able to advise further on the type of material which might be available. Schools, churches, clubs and commercial organisations may have published magazines featuring letters from those on active service and keeping their readers up to date with the activities and whereabouts of their friends and colleagues. This is a source of information which is often neglected, possibly because it does involve very time-consuming research. The **British Library Newspaper Library, Colindale Avenue, London NW9 5HE** has copies of newspapers from all over the country. You can gain access to their catalogue online at **www.bl.uk/collections/newspapers.html** The recent increase in interest in family history and the world wars has led to many new publications about war memorials and the local citizens who served. The Department of Printed Books actively seeks to acquire this kind of material (and we are always grateful to have works of this nature brought to our notice).

Some published squadron histories contain rolls of honour. While new squadron histories continue to appear, it should be noted that the number of such histories remains relatively small in comparison with the total number of squadrons which have existed in the history of the Royal Air Force.

Some rolls of honour can be found on leaflets or programmes relating to the building and unveiling of war memorials. The Imperial War Museum launched an appeal shortly after the end of the First World War for this type of information and the Department of Printed Books has a large ephemera collection relating to war memorials, whilst the Photograph Archive has photographs.

UNITED KINGDOM NATIONAL INVENTORY OF WAR MEMORIALS

The **United Kingdom National Inventory of War Memorials** based at the Imperial War Museum is compiling a listing of all war memorials in the United Kingdom. You can conduct a search at the website **www.ukniwm.org.uk**

The initial aim of the project was to record the memorials, but in some cases, the names and additional material were sent to the UKNIWM. The names have now been input onto a searchable 'virtual memorial' that can be added to by members of the public, in conjunction with Channel 4. You can find this database at **www.channel4.com/history/microsites/L/lostgeneration/index.html**

The UKNIWM is always interested to learn of any memorial that might not have already been recorded.

MEDICAL RECORDS

Very few medical records have survived from the First World War – most were destroyed in 1975, since it was felt that as all those liable to claim pensions were now receiving old age pensions the records were no longer needed. Those records retained as a sample are now held in record class *MH 106* at The National Archives. Most of the records in this class relate to the Army, but a few for the Royal Flying Corps are included.

General information on the organisation and operation of Army medical services during the First World War can be found in the four-volume official history by Macpherson. The official history of the RAF medical services in the Second World War, edited by SC Rexford-Welch, consists of three volumes dealing respectively with administration, commands and campaigns. The campaigns volume has a number of index references to hospitals and medical units. For both world wars there are also official medical histories relating to more technical aspects such as surgery and pathology. The Department of Printed Books holds a good selection of titles relating to various different aspects of health and medicine in both world wars, such as shellshock and tropical medicine, and the work of doctors and nurses in different medical establishments.

The Department of Printed Books also holds a set of *War Office Weekly Casualty Lists* from August 1917 to February 1919 which contain references to killed, wounded and captured servicemen. This is a difficult and unrewarding source to use. No specific dates are given other than the general issue date of the *List* and entries have been proven to appear several months after the occasion to which they refer.

Throughout the First World War the Enquiry for the Wounded and Missing Department of the British Red Cross and Order of St John issued monthly *Enquiry Lists* with fortnightly supplements. These were listings of wounded and missing officers and men, compiled from official and unofficial sources, for use by searchers in the United Kingdom and abroad. In the sections for the Royal Flying Corps/Royal Air Force and the Royal Naval Air Service the missing are listed by squadron and by date. Of the fifty volumes produced between 1915 and 1919 only a few have survived and the Department of Printed Books holds the following issues:

> [February 1915]; 18 May 1915; 26 June 1915; 17 July 1915, supplement B; 24 July 1915, supplement B; 31 July 1915, supplement B; 7 August 1915, supplement B; 14 August 1915, supplement B; 4 September 1915; 18 September 1915, supplement no. 2; 1 February 1916; 15 September 1916, supplement [photocopy]; 1 August 1917, no. 14 [1989 reprint by Sunset Militaria and Ray Westlake]; 1 October 1918, no. 17; 1 December 1918, no. 21.

The **Department of Research and Information Services** at the **Royal Air Force Museum, Grahame Park Way, London NW9 5LL** holds several series of official casualty records but although detailed these records are not complete.

PRISONERS OF WAR

Records of prisoners of war were compiled by each national branch of the Red Cross and are now all held centrally by the **Archives Division and Research Service, International Committee of the Red Cross, 19 Avenue de la Paix, Geneva CH-1202, Switzerland**. Because of their personal nature, these records are not accessible to the general public but paid searches can be conducted (currently 80 Swiss Francs an hour) – please be patient as this may take some time. You will need to know the **full name** and **nationality** of the individual you are researching. Additional details such as unit, number, place and date of birth, date of capture and name of father are likely to aid your enquiry. More information is available on the website at **www.icrc.org/eng** (click on Info Resources, and then ICRC Information Services – an electronic application form can be found under Archives).

FIRST WORLD WAR

Records held at The National Archives that may be of assistance include *AIR 1* and *FO 383*. Record class *WO 161* may be the most useful, and you can find an index to this (although not the records themselves) on *The Long, Long Trail* website at **www.1914-1918.net/POW/index.php**

The Department of Printed Books has a copy of the *List of British Officers Taken Prisoner in the Various Theatres of War Between August 1914 and November 1918*, compiled by the military agents Cox and Co in 1919. However, this will only be useful if you are seeking an individual who was commissioned.

There is no comparable listing for other ranks, but the *Enquiry Lists and War Office Weekly Casualty Lists* may prove helpful. Trevor Henshaw's *The Sky their Battlefield: Air Fighting and the Complete List of Allied Air Casualties from Enemy Action in the First War: British, Commonwealth, and United States Air Services 1914 to 1918* will also provide some information if an individual mentioned in this was taken prisoner.

Mrs Pope-Hennessey compiled a map gazetteer showing the principal Central Powers prisoner of war camps in Germany and Austria called *Map of the Main Prison Camps in Germany and Austria*. It was originally published by Nisbet and Co during the First World War, and has recently been reprinted – it can be purchased from the Imperial War Museum for £5.00.

Although not many books relating to First World War prisoners are listed in the bibliography you can find material on this period at the Imperial War Museum. Have a look at the different Museum catalogues available on **Collections Online** at **www.iwmcollections.org.uk**

SECOND WORLD WAR

The recently released *Liberated Prisoner of War Interrogation Questionaires* held at The National Archives in record class *WO 344* may be one of the most useful sources available. Other potential helpful record classes include *AIR 2*, *AIR 14*, *AIR 20* and *WO 208*.

Published sources available in the Department of Printed Books include volume three of a three volume work reprinted by John

Hayward: *Prisoners of War: Naval and Air Forces of Great Britain and the Empire, 1939-1945: Alphabetical Nominal Registers (including Number, Rank/Rating, POW Number and Camp Location Details) listing over 21,000 Australian, British, Canadian, New Zealand, South African and other Naval and Air Force Prisoners of War of All Ranks held in Germany and German Occupied Territories… (all Lists Corrected Generally up to 30th March 1945).*

Two excellent sources covering RAF prisoners are *Footprints on the Sands of Time: RAF Bomber Command Prisoners-of-War in Germany 1939-1945* by Oliver Clutton-Brock (Grub Street, London, 2003) and *Unsung Heroes of the Royal Air Force: the Far East Prisoners of War 1941-1945* by Les and Pam Stubbs (Barry Books, Grantham, Lincolnshire, 2002).

Probably the best single volume work dealing with POWs generally is *Official History of New Zealand in the Second World War, 1939 - 1945: Prisoners of War* by W Wynne Mason (War History Branch, Department of Internal Affairs, Wellington, New Zealand, 1954). You will find some other key works listed in the bibliography, and should be aware that the Department of Printed Books has autobiographies, general works about prisoners of war, escape attempts and some titles relating to specific camps. The Department of Documents and Sound Archive may also have relevant personal accounts.

Issues of *The Prisoner of War: the Official Organ of the Prisoners of War Department of the Red Cross and St John War Organisation* contain interesting background information, particularly about activities in POW camps in Occupied Europe.

You may also be interested in the **Royal Air Forces Ex-POW Association** website at **www.rafinfo.org.uk/rafexpow** Other websites that might also be helpful are the **National Ex-Prisoner of War Association** at **http://prisonerofwar.freeservers.com** and the **Children of Far East Prisoners of War** at **www.cofepow.org.uk**

ADDITIONAL SOURCES

OFFICIAL SOURCES

Official documentation of various kinds, including the operations record books of squadrons and other units, is now with The National Archives. The most relevant Air Historical Branch files are *AIR 1* and *AIR 2* for the First World War and *AIR 5* and *AIR 9* for the inter-war era. The operations record books of squadrons during the Second World War are included in *AIR 27*. Operations Record Books (Form 540) and their appendixes (Form 541) were a record of daily events kept by all branches of the RAF and can be extremely detailed. The Operations Record Books of Commands, Groups, Wings, Squadrons, Stations and miscellaneous units can be found in other *AIR* record classes.

PUBLISHED SOURCES

Many books have been published dealing with the history of the RAF, its commands and squadrons and its operations from the First World War to the present day. Most of these can be consulted by appointment in the Department of Printed Books Reading Room, and we are always happy to advise about what might be available on specific subject areas. Some of the standard reference works on the RAF are listed in Appendix IV. While new squadron histories continue to be published the number of such histories remains relatively small when compared to the total number of squadrons which have existed during the course of the RAF's history.

While some aspects and campaigns are well covered, others are not particularly well documented in published sources. In comparison with fighter operations on the Western Front during the First World War, reconnaissance and ground support operations are less well covered. There are many books on the Battle of Britain and quite a large number on Bomber Command and the strategic air offensive against Germany during the Second World War. The air war against Japan is less well documented than the air war against Germany.

Recent publications may have superseded older ones as they are able to make use of historical material which was previously unavailable to authors and historians in past years. A modern approach is for publishers such as Grub Street to produce narrative histories which describe events in a systematic chronological way; these usually include very detailed indexes making them excellent reference books.

Some books which deal more indirectly with the RAF may nevertheless be useful to the researcher. There are a limited number of published rolls of honour relating to RAF awards. Some of the many books concerned with particular aircraft types and manufacturers (such as those published by Putnam) can also provide helpful information.

In recent years there has been increasing interest in airfield history. The ten-volume series *Action Stations* published by Patrick Stephens contains brief histories of all the former military airfields in Great Britain and Northern Ireland. There are also a number of other works produced by various publishers and local historians, some dealing with a number of airfields in a particular area and others being histories of individual airfields. An extremely detailed journal called *Airfield Review* is produced by the Airfield Research Group, and will prove of interest to those wishing to find out more about this aspect of RAF history. For anybody wishing to experience what an RAF airfield was like, a trip to Imperial War Museum Duxford (formerly RAF Duxford) is a must! Naturally a large variety of aircraft can be seen there, but also such elements of daily life as the chapel and guardroom, and the vast expanses of windswept land.

JOURNALS

Airmail, magazine of the **Royal Air Forces Association**, and the commercially published monthlies *Flypast* and *Aeroplane Monthly* from time to time publish appeals from readers on aviation history topics including the contacting and tracing of former RAF personnel. (There may be lengthy waiting lists for the publication of such appeals). The addresses for these magazines are: *Airmail*, **RAFATRAD Ltd, Unit 3, 5 Sybron Way, Millbrook Industrial Estate, Crowborough, East Sussex TN6 3DZ**, *Flypast*, **Key Publishing Ltd, PO Box 100, Stamford, Lincolnshire PE9 1XQ** and *Aeroplane Monthly*, **King's Reach Tower, Stamford Street, London SE1 9LS**.

The **Royal British Legion, 48 Pall Mall, London SW1Y 5JY** should not be forgotten. Their magazine *Legion*, and also their website, carry a column called 'Lost Trails' which can help with tracing people.

There are a number of other service and ex-service publications which might offer a similar service or may increase your knowledge of certain subject areas – details of some appropriate publications should be available from the Department of Printed Books.

A useful publication for First World War enthusiasts, which might be helpful for sharing research interests, is *Cross and Cockade International Journal*, **c/o Mick Davis, 4 Cliff Terrace, Easington, Peterlee, County Durham SR8 3BL**.

UNPUBLISHED SOURCES

The Department of Printed Books has a good collection of autobiographical and biographical material, but there are additional sources for this type of information. Other reference departments in the Museum will prove very helpful for adding to the personal experience element of conflict. Letters and diaries as well as unpublished reminiscences are actively collected by the Department of Documents, and as the Department of Printed Books and Documents share a reading room it is very easy to make appointments to consult both departmental holdings at the same time. The Sound Archive have recordings of interviews made with veterans and again these can be of great assistance. The Photograph Archive should also be consulted as it is possible that you may be able to find pictures of interest. The Archive has an excellent collection of photographs of aircraft, although views of stations or squadrons may be harder to find.

MAGAZINES

Family history has become extremely popular in recent years and there are many magazines on the market which offer advice and guidance. The Imperial War Museum has subscribed to *Family Tree Magazine* since 1989, (back copies can be consulted in our Reading Room), but there have been many new publications of this sort produced in recent years. *Family Tree Magazine* is published monthly by **ABM Publishing Ltd, 61 Great Whyte, Ramsey, Huntingdon, Cambridgeshire PE26 1HJ**. Other titles include *Family History News and Digest* produced by the Federation of Family History Societies, *Genealogists Magazine* by the Society of Genealogists, *Ancestors* published by The National Archives and *Family History Monthly.* Contact details for all these can be found in Appendix III.

SOCIETIES

Genealogical societies, such as the **Federation of Family History Societies, c/o FFHS Administrator, PO Box 2425, Coventry CV5 6YX** and the **Society of Genealogists, 14 Charterhouse Buildings, Goswell Road, London EC1M 7BA**, may be able to offer advice, as well as provide details of local societies and organisations. There are all sorts of societies concentrating on local areas, individual names, occupations, nationalities, etc. Both the Federation of Family History Societies and the Society of Genealogists have produced useful guides for the family historian, some of which are listed in Appendix IV.

LOCAL LIBRARIES AND ARCHIVES

Information held in your relative's home area should not be overlooked. Sources such as local histories, rolls of honour and newspapers, described in the Casualty Records section, can be excellent sources. One other often overlooked but potentially helpful resource is the Absent Voters List, detailed below.

The Family and Local History Handbook, published annually, is full of genealogical and historical articles of interest to the beginner and experienced researcher alike. It also contains contact details for a wide variety of registrars of births, marriages and deaths, record offices, libraries, museums and societies.

An online listing of record repositories can be found at **www.nationalarchives.gov.uk/archon**
The National Register of Archives – available online at **www.nationalarchives.gov.uk/nra** – will allow some searching of archival catalogues. Details about family and local history resources located in public libraries, together with contact details, can be found at **www.familia.org.uk**

ABSENT VOTERS LISTS

Some basic information should also be found in either the Absent Voters Lists of 1918 or the Service Voters Registers of 1945, although this does assume that the soldier was alive or in service at the date they were compiled. These were produced in order to enable servicemen, over the age of 21, to vote in the constituency of their home address, and should be located in the local studies collection of the relevant library service or county record office.

A few Absent Voters Lists from the First World War can now be found on the internet.

Online Absent Voters Lists:

Accrington: **www.pals.org.uk/avl/index.htm**

Grimsby and Cleethorpes:
www.angelfire.com/de/delighted/voters.html

Leeds: **www.leeds.gov.uk** [search under Online Databases]

Wakefield:
www.wakefieldfhs.org.uk/abscent%20voters.htm

To find out what is held in the area your relative came from, and how to gain access to it, you can check on the website **www.familia.org.uk**

THE INTERNET

The internet has revolutionised family history research, and there are many websites that can help you, either by giving advice, helping with a specific subject, or allowing you to contact individuals or appeal for information. Not everything that appears on the internet is current or correct information, and you should always check to see who has created the website and what their aim is. Some website addresses can be found in Appendix III, but you should be aware that websites sometimes just disappear, and that new ones are springing into life all the time. Following links from one site to another can often be a rewarding activity, if sometimes frustrating.

An excellent site for those who are starting out is **www.familyrecords.gov.uk** as this explains what records you can expect to find and how to locate them, as well as giving links. Other sites that might be helpful are Cyndi's List at **www.cyndislist.com** and GENUKI at **www.genuki.org.uk**

For tracing ex-servicemen and women, there are a number of websites that you can contact. The Royal British Legion website at **www.britishlegion.org.uk** features a 'Lost Trails' section. A couple of other sites are MOD Reunited at **www.modreunited.com** and Forces Reunited at **www.forcesreunited.org.uk**

FAMILY HISTORY FAIRS

Family History fairs are held regularly around the country, and can be excellent places for both beginners and experienced researchers to find out what is available. The Imperial War Museum does sometimes participate in larger fairs, and also regularly has family history days in the Museum galleries. Visitors are welcome to come and ask questions, and staff are able to spend longer dealing with these than we are in the normal course of our work. The Museum website family history pages has details of the dates of these events.

APPENDIX I

OFFICIAL NUMBERING

Very little information is available on the subject of Royal Flying Corps and Royal Air Force service numbers. Men who joined the RFC between its formation in 1912 and August 1914 had the service numbers 1 to 1400 and are listed in *A Contemptible Little Flying Corps* by JV Webb and I McInnes (see Appendix IV).

The numbers in the first volume of the 1918 *Muster Roll* (which lists NCOs and other ranks only) go up to 102,941. The holder of this number joined in December 1917. The numbers in the second volume range from 102,942 to 223,200. The dates of joining are given in every case but these are not in a strict chronological order which correlates with the numbers. The numbers in the third and final volume of the *Muster Roll* go from 223,201 to 409,095. The dates of joining range from May 1917 to March 1918 but again they do not appear to follow a strict chronological order.

Royal Navy service numbers used by the Royal Naval Air Service had the prefix 'F'. When the men transferred into the RAF in 1918, their RNAS service numbers were adapted to bring them into line with the numbers being used in the new service. The F prefix was removed and the number 2 and as many noughts as necessary were added in front of the old RNAS number to make it six digits eg F1002 became 201,002 or F54559 became 254,559. Some Royal Navy personnel who had transferred into the RNAS on its formation in July 1914 retained their RN service numbers. Those pre-July 1914 sailors who went on to serve in the RAF in 1918 were given service numbers within the 313,001 and 316,000 range.

Officers' numbers were published in the *Air Force List* from September 1939. They do not appear in the main body of the list but are included in the index. However, not all the names in the index have numbers against them. All the numbers given consist of five digits, but in some cases the first of these is a 0. By January 1945 all officers had numbers of either five or six digits. To take a representative example from the middle of the war, an airman commissioned as a Pilot Officer in August 1943 had the number 147,174.

Officers and airmen of the Commonwealth air forces had numbers preceded by a letter prefix:
Australia – 'Aus.', Canada – 'J' or 'C' (officers) and 'R' (other ranks) and New Zealand – 'NZ'. The exception was the South African Air Force which had its own separate numbering system.

In the post-1945 era RAF officers' numbers have gone up to seven digits.

Judging from the entries in the Commonwealth War Graves Commission registers for the Second World War the NCOs and airmen whose deaths are recorded had service numbers of either six or seven digits. The seven-digit numbers all appear to begin with the number 1.

With regard to commissioning from the ranks in the RAF, there have been two systems in operation, depending on when it occurred. Prior to 1947 a new service number was issued on commissioning. After that date the same service number was retained. However, in addition to the numbers an alphabetical prefix or suffix is included: an airman's service number has the letter as a prefix, whereas the letter is a suffix to an officer's service number.

APPENDIX II

ABBREVIATIONS

GENERAL

AAC	Army Air Corps
AAF	Auxiliary Air Force
AAFRO	Auxiliary Air Force Reserve of Officers
AASF	Advanced Air Striking Force
ACAS	Assistant Chief of Air Staff
ACIs	Air Council Instructions
ADGB	Air Defence of Great Britain
AG	Air Gunner
AHB	Air Historical Branch
ALG	Advanced Landing Ground
AM	Air Ministry
AMOs	Air Ministry Orders
AOC	Air Officer Commanding
AP	Air Publication
ASR	Air Sea Rescue
ATA	Air Transport Auxiliary
ATC	Air Training Corps
BCATP	British Commonwealth Air Training Plan
BEF	British Expeditionary Force
CAS	Chief of Air Staff
CO	Commanding Officer (There was only one CO on any unit or station, ie the most senior rank appointed)
CS	Continuous Service
CWGC	Commonwealth War Graves Commission
DCAS	Deputy Chief of Air Staff

EFTS	Elementary Flying Training School
FAA	Fleet Air Arm
FEAF	Far East Air Force
FEPOW	Far East Prisoner of War
FTR	Failed To Return
FTS	Flying Training School
HCU	Heavy Conversion Unit (ie on to four-engined aircraft)
HE	High Explosive
HM	His Majesty's/Her Majesty's
HQ	Headquarters
I/C	In Charge of (as in 'Officer in charge of ...')
IF	Independent Force
ITW	Initial Training Wing
IWGC	Imperial War Graves Commission
KRs	King's Regulations
LG	Landing Ground
MAP	Ministry of Aircraft Production
MO	Medical Officer
MOD	Ministry of Defence
MT	Mechanical Transport; later, Motor Transport
MU	Maintenance Unit
NAAFI	Navy, Army and Air Force Institute
NATO	North Atlantic Treaty Organisation
NCO	Non-Commissioned Officer
OC	Officer Commanding (An OC might be a senior officer commanding a Wing or Squadron, but might also be a very junior officer given specific 'secondary duties'. Not the same as CO)
OCTU	Officer Cadet Training Unit

ORB	Operations Record Book
OTU	Operational Training Unit
PFF	Path Finder Force (No. 8 Group, Bomber Command)
PMRAFNS	Princess Mary's Royal Air Force Nursing Service
POW	Prisoner of War
PRO	Public Record Office
PRU	Photographic Reconnaissance Unit
RAAF	Royal Australian Air Force
RAuxAF	Royal Auxiliary Air Force
RAE	Royal Aircraft Establishment (Farnborough)
RAF	Royal Air Force
RAFO	Reserve of Air Force Officers
RAFVR	Royal Air Force Volunteer Reserve
RCAF	Royal Canadian Air Force
RDF	Radio Direction Finding (original cover name for radar)
RFC	Royal Flying Corps
RIAF	Royal Indian Air Force
RN	Royal Navy/Royal Naval
RNAS	Royal Naval Air Service
RND	Royal Naval Division
RNZAF	Royal New Zealand Air Force
ROC	Royal Observer Corps
R/T	Radio Telephony
SAAF	South African Air Force
SASO	Senior Air Staff Officer
SD	Special Duties
SFTS	Service Flying Training School
SNCO	Senior Non-Commissioned Officer
SOC	Struck Off Charge

TAF	Tactical Air Force
TNA	The National Archives
U/S	Unserviceable
USAAF	United States Army Air Forces (up to 1947)
USAF	United States Air Force (from 1947)
VAD	Voluntary Aid Detachment
VCAS	Vice Chief of the Air Staff
WAAF	Women's Auxiliary Air Force
WOP	Wireless Operator
WOP/AG	Wireless Operator/Air Gunner
WRAF	Women's Royal Air Force
W/T	Wireless Telegraphy

RANKS

AC, A/Cdr or Air Cdre	Air Commodore
AC1	Aircraftman 1st Class
AC2	Aircraftman 2nd Class
ACM	Air Chief Marshal
ACW1	Aircraftwoman 1st Class
ACW2	Aircraftwoman 2nd Class
AM or Air Mshl	Air Marshal
AVM	Air Vice Marshal
Chf Tech	Chief Technician
Cpl	Corporal
F/L, F/Lt or Flt Lt	Flight Lieutenant
F/O or Fg Off	Flying Officer
F/S or F/Sgt	Flight Sergeant
G/C or Gp Capt	Group Captain
Jnr Tech	Junior Technician
LAC	Leading Aircraftman
LACW	Leading Aircraftwoman

MAcr	Master Aircrew
MRAF	Marshal of the Royal Air Force
P/O or Plt Off	Pilot Officer
SAC	Senior Aircraftman
Sgt	Sergeant
S/L or Sqn Ldr	Squadron Leader
W/C or Wg Cdr	Wing Commander
W/O or WO	Warrant Officer
WO2	Warrant Officer 2nd Class

HONOURS AND AWARDS

AE	Air Efficiency Award
AFC	Air Force Cross
AFM	Air Force Medal
BEM	British Empire Medal
CB	Companion of the Bath
CBE	Commander of the Order of the British Empire
CGC	Conspicuous Gallantry Cross
CGM	Conspicuous Gallantry Medal
DCM	Distinguished Conduct Medal
DFC	Distinguished Flying Cross
DFM	Distinguished Flying Medal
DSC	Distinguished Service Cross
DSM	Distinguished Service Medal
DSO	Distinguished Service Order
GC	George Cross
GM	George Medal
GSM	General Service Medal
LS & GCM	Long Service and Good Conduct Medal
MBE	Member of the Order of the British Empire

MC	Military Cross
MID	Mention in Despatches
MM	Military Medal
MSM	Meritorious Service Medal
OBE	Order of the British Empire
QGM	Queen's Gallantry Medal
RRC	Royal Red Cross
VC	Victoria Cross

These are a selection only of the most commonly used abbreviations. Listings of abbreviations can also be found in issues of the *Air Force List*, a run of which is held by the Department of Printed Books. Some abbreviations will also be found in many of the books listed in the bibliography. In addition the Department holds several published guides to abbreviations in use at various times during the 20th Century.

APPENDIX III

USEFUL ADDRESSES

MINISTRY OF DEFENCE

Joint Casualty and Compassionate Centre
Armed Forces Personnel Administration Agency, Building 182,
RAF Innsworth, Gloucester GL3 1HW
[RAF personnel buried in publicly funded 'non World War' graves]

Ministry of Defence, Air Historical Branch
Building 266, RAF Bentley Priory, Stanmore, Middlesex HA7 3HH
[RAF casualties and aircraft losses - Second World War onwards]

Ministry of Defence Medal Office
Building 250, RAF Innsworth, Gloucester GL3 1HW
[campaign, long service and gallantry medal enquiries and medal claims]

RAF Disclosure of Information Office
PMA IM 1B (RAF), Room 5, Building 248A, RAF Personnel Management Agency, RAF Innsworth, Gloucester GL3 1EZ
[service records - mid 1920s to date]

MUSEUMS, ARCHIVES AND RECORD OFFICES

British Library Newspaper Library
Colindale Avenue, London NW9 5HE
Tel: 020 7412 7353
www.bl.uk/collections/newspapers.html

Commonwealth War Graves Commission
2 Marlow Road, Maidenhead, Berkshire SL6 7DX
Tel: 01628 634221
www.cwgc.org

Family Records Centre
1 Myddelton Street, London EC1R 1UW
Tel: 020 8392 5300
www.familyrecords.gov.uk/frc/

Fleet Air Arm Museum
Centre for Naval Aviation Records and Research, Box D6, RNAS Yeovilton, Yeovil, near Ilchester, Somerset BA22 8HT
Tel: 01935 840565
www.fleetairarm.com

General Register Office
PO Box 2, Southport, Merseyside PR8 2JD
Tel: 0845 603 7788
www.gro.gov.uk

General Register Office (Dublin)
Government Offices, Covent Road, Roscommon, Eire
Tel: 090 663 2900
www.groireland.ie

General Register Office (Northern Ireland)

Oxford House, 49-55 Chichester Street, Belfast, Northern Ireland BT1 4HL

Tel: 028 9025 2000

www.groni.gov.uk

General Register Office for Scotland

New Register House, 3 West Register Street, Edinburgh EH1 3YT

Tel: 0131 334 0380

www.gro-scotland.gov.uk/

Guildhall Library

Aldermanbury, London EC2P 2EJ

Tel: 020 7332 1868

www.cityoflondon.gov.uk/search_guildhall

International Committee of the Red Cross

Archives Division and Research Service, 19 Avenue de la Paix, Geneva CH-1202, Switzerland

www.icrc.org/eng

The National Archives

Ruskin Avenue, Kew, Richmond, Surrey TW9 4DU

Tel: 020 8876 3444

www.nationalarchives.gov.uk

Royal Air Force Museum

Department of Research and Information Services, Grahame Park Way, London NW9 5LL

Tel: 020 8205 2266

www.rafmuseum.org.uk

Information on other museums and archives can be found in the annual publications *The World of Learning* and *The Museums Yearbook*, available at most libraries and information centres.

SOCIETIES, ASSOCIATIONS AND PERIODICALS

Aeroplane Monthly
King's Reach Tower, Stamford Street, London SE1 9LS
www.aeroplanemonthly.com

Airfield Review
Airfield Research Group, Hon Gen Sec: Raymond Towler, 33A Earls Street, Thetford, Norfolk IP24 2AB
www.airfield-research-group.co.uk/home.htm

Airmail
RAFATRAD Ltd, Unit 3, 5 Sybron Way, Millbrook Industrial Estate, Crowborough, East Sussex TN6 3DZ
Tel: 01892 600192

Ancestors
PO Box 38, Richmond TW9 4AJ
www.ancestorsmagazine.co.uk

British, Commonwealth and Polish Air Services Personnel Archive
c/o G Negus Esq, 2 Heathcote Avenue, Solihull, West Midlands B91 1QL
www.rquirk.com/negus.html
[The Archive is a computer-based, non-government record of over 116,000 air force fatalities in several categories. While not as comprehensive as the CWGC's records, it differs from them in several significant ways. UK enquirers are requested to supply a large sae and those from overseas

are requested to supply international reply coupons. The Archive is a spare-time activity – patience and donations are greatly appreciated.]

Cross and Cockade International Journal
c/o Mick Davis, 4 Cliff Terrace, Easington, Peterlee, County Durham SR8 3BL
www.crossandcockade.com

Family History Monthly
The Metropolis Group, 140 Wales Farm Road, London W3 6UG
www.metropolis.co.uk/familyhistory.html

Family Tree Magazine
ABM Publishing Ltd, 61 Great Whyte, Ramsey, Huntingdon, Cambridgeshire PE26 1HJ
Tel: 01487 814050
www.family-tree.co.uk

Federation of Family History Societies
FFHS Administrator, PO Box 2425, Coventry CV5 6YX
Publishes *Family History News and Digest: the Official Journal of the Federation of Family History Societies*
www.ffhs.org.uk

Flypast
Key Publishing Ltd, PO Box 100, Stamford, Lincolnshire PE9 1XQ
Tel: 01780 755131
www.flypast.com

Legion Magazine
Royal British Legion, 48 Pall Mall, London SW1Y 5JY
www.britishlegion.org.uk

Royal Air Forces Association

Central Headquarters, 117½ Loughborough Road, Leicester LE4 5ND

Tel: 0116 266 5224

www.rafa.org.uk

Society of Genealogists

14 Charterhouse Buildings, Goswell Road, London EC1M 7BA

Publishes *Genealogists Magazine*

Tel: 020 7251 8799

www.sog.org.uk

WAAF Association

c/o Secretary: Mrs Florence Mahoney, 91 Marina Avenue, New Malden, Surrey KT3 6NG

www.waafassociation.org.uk

SOME HELPFUL WEBSITES

BCAUR: British & Commonwealth Air Unit Register

http://associations.rafinfo.org.uk/

Children of Far East Prisoners of War

www.cofepow.org.uk

National Ex-Prisoner of War Association

http://prisonerofwar.freeservers.com

Princess Mary's Royal Air Force Nursing Service

www.pmrafns.org

Royal Air Force

www.raf.mod.uk

Royal Air Force Reserves

www.rafreserves.com

Royal Air Forces Ex-POW Association

www.rafinfo.org.uk/rafexpow

Scots at War

www.fettes.com/scotsatwar

All contact details in this publication were correct at the time of printing.

APPENDIX IV

SELECT BIBLIOGRAPHY

The majority of the books listed below are held by the Department of Printed Books and can be consulted in the Reading Room – 24 hours notice of an intended visit should be given. Alternative copies may be available through the inter-library loan scheme – please enquire at your local library. Some titles will be out of print, but may be available through second-hand and specialist book dealers.

The bibliography has been divided into the following subject areas: Helpful books for family historians (p. 72), General books about RAF operations, organisation and life (p. 74), Medals and Awards (p. 88), Casualties, rolls of honour and memorials (p. 91) and Prisoners of War (p. 96).

HELPFUL BOOKS FOR FAMILY HISTORIANS

BEVAN, Amanda
Tracing your Ancestors in the Public Record Office by Amanda Bevan.
6th ed.; Public Record Office, Richmond, Surrey, 2002.
(Public Record Office Handbook; no. 19)
ISBN 1-903365-34-1 (pbk.)

COLWELL, Stella
The Family Records Centre: a User's Guide by Stella Colwell.
2nd ed.; Public Record Office, Richmond, Surrey, 2002.
(Public Record Office Readers' Guide; no. 17)
ISBN 1-903365-36-8 (pbk.)

FOWLER, Simon
Tracing Your First World War Ancestors by Simon Fowler.
Countryside Books, Newbury, Berkshire, 2003.
ISBN 1-85306-791-1 (pbk.)

SPENCER, William
Air Force Records for Family Historians by William Spencer.
Public Record Office, Richmond, Surrey, 2000.
(Public Record Office Readers' Guide; no. 21)
ISBN 1-873162-93-6 (pbk.)

SPENCER, William
Army Service Records of the First World War by William Spencer.
3rd rev. ed.; Public Record Office, Richmond, Surrey, 2001.
(Public Record Office Readers' Guide: no. 19)
ISBN 1-903365-55-3 (pbk.)

WILSON, Eunice
The Records of the Royal Air Force: how to find the Few by Eunice Wilson.
Federation of Family History Societies, Birmingham, 1991.
ISBN 1-872094-17-1 (pbk.)

GENERAL BOOKS ABOUT RAF ORGANISATION, OPERATIONS AND LIFE

FIRST WORLD WAR

AIR MINISTRY
The Royal Air Force in the Great War compiled by the Air Ministry.
Imperial War Museum, Department of Printed Books, London, 1996.
ISBN 1-870423-70-4
[3rd revised edition originally published in 1936 under the title *A Short History of the Royal Air Force*]

BOWYER, Chaz
Royal Flying Corps Communiqués 1917-1918 edited by Chaz Bowyer.
Grub Street, London, 1998.
ISBN 1-898697-79-5

COLE, Christopher
The Air Defence of Britain, 1914-1918 by Christopher Cole and EF Cheesman.
Putnam, London, 1984.
ISBN 0-370-30538-3

COLE, Christopher
Royal Air Force 1918 edited by Christopher Cole.
William Kimber, London, 1968.

COLE, Christopher
Royal Flying Corps 1915-1916 edited by Christopher Cole.
William Kimber, London, 1969.
ISBN 0-7183-0261-3

RALEIGH, Walter
The War in the Air: being the Story of the Part Played in the Great War by the Royal Air Force. *[Volumes I - VI and Appendices]* by Walter Raleigh [and] HA Jones.
Imperial War Museum, Department of Printed Books, London, 1997-1999.
(History of the Great War based on Official Documents)
[facsimile of original editions dating from 1922-1937]

STEEL, Nigel
Tumult in the Clouds: the British Experience of the War in the Air 1914-1918 by Nigel Steel and Peter Hart.
Hodder and Stoughton, London, 1997.
ISBN 0-340-63845-1

STURTIVANT, Ray
Royal Navy Aircraft Serials and Units, 1911 to 1919 by Ray Sturtivant and Gordon Page.
Air Britain, Tonbridge, Kent, 1992.
ISBN 0-85130-191-6

WINTER, Denis
The First of the Few: Fighter Pilots of the First World War by Denis Winter.
Allen Lane, London, 1982.
ISBN 0-7139-1278-2

INTER-WAR

BOWYER, Chaz
RAF Operations, 1918-38 by Chaz Bowyer.
William Kimber, London, 1988.
ISBN 0-7183-0671-6

JAMES, John
The Paladins: a Social History of the RAF up to the Outbreak of World War II by John James.
Macdonald, London, 1990.
ISBN 0-356-19071-4

PHILPOTT, Ian M
The Royal Air Force: An Encyclopedia of the Inter-War Years: Volume I: the Trenchard Years, 1918 to 1929 by Wing Commander Ian M Philpott.
Pen and Sword Aviation, Barnsley, South Yorkshire, 2005.
ISBN 1-88415-154-9

SECOND WORLD WAR

BISHOP, Patrick
Fighter Boys: Saving Britain, 1940 by Patrick Bishop.
HarperCollins, London, 2003.
ISBN 0-00-257169-2

BOWYER, Chaz
Royal Air Force Handbook 1939-1945 by Chaz Bowyer.
Ian Allan, London, 1984.
ISBN 0-7110-1318-7

BOWYER, Michael JF
2 Group R.A.F.: a Complete History 1936-1945 by Michael JF Bowyer.
Faber and Faber, London, 1974.
ISBN 0-571-09491-0

CULL, Brian
Hurricanes over Malta, June 1940-April 1942 by Brian Cull and Frederick Galea.
Rev. ed.; Grub Street, London, 2001.
ISBN 1-902304-91-8

FALCONER, Jonathan
The Bomber Command Handbook, 1939-1945 by Jonathan Falconer.
Sutton, Stroud, Gloucestershire, 1998.
ISBN 0-7509-1819-5

FOREMAN, John
Air War 1941: the Turning Point: the Day by Day Account of Air Operations over Northwest Europe: [2 volumes] by John Foreman.
Air Research Publications, Walton-on-Thames, Surrey, 1993-1994.
ISBN Part 1: 1-871187-22-2
ISBN Part 2: 1-871187-27-3

FOREMAN, John
The Fighter Command War Diaries: the Operational History of Fighter Command, Second Tactical Air Force, 100 Group and Air Defence of Great Britain 1939-45 by John Foreman.
Air Research Publications, Walton-on-Thames, Surrey, 1996-2002.
ISBN 1-871187-44-3. Vol. 1 : September 1939 to September 1940
ISBN 1-871187-35-4. Vol. 2 : September 1940 to December 1941
ISBN 1-871187-39-7. Vol. 3 : January 1942 to June 1943
ISBN 1-871187-43-5. Vol. 4 : July 1943 to June 1944
ISBN 1-871187-45-1. Vol. 5 : July 1944 to May 1945

MIDDLEBROOK, Martin
The Berlin Raids: R.A.F. Bomber Command Winter 1943-44 by Martin Middlebrook.
Viking, London, 1988.
ISBN 0-670-80697-8

MIDDLEBROOK, Martin
The Bomber Command War Diaries: an Operational Reference Book 1939-1945 by Martin Middlebrook and Chris Everitt.
Rev. ed.; Midland Publishing, Leicester, 1996.
ISBN 1-85780-033-8 (pbk.)

PHILLIPS, J Alwyn
The Valley of the Shadow of Death: an Account of the Royal Air Force Bomber Command Night Bombing and Minelaying Operations including 'the Battle of the Ruhr', March 5th/6th to July 18th/19th 1943 by J Alwyn Phillips.
Air Research Publications, New Malden, Surrey, 1992.
ISBN 1-87118-713-3

PROBERT, Henry
The Forgotten Air Force: the Royal Air Force in the War Against Japan, 1941-1945 by Henry Probert.
Brassey's, London, 1995.
ISBN 1-85753-065-9

RICHARDS, Denis
Royal Air Force 1939-1945. Volumes I-III by Denis Richards and Hilary St George Saunders.
HMSO, London, 1953-1954.

ROLFE, Mel

Bomber Boys by Mel Rolfe.

Grub Street, London, 2004.

ISBN 1-904010-86-5

SHORES, Christopher

2nd Tactical Air Force by Christopher Shores and Chris Thomas.

Rev. ed.; Classic Publications, Hersham, Surrey, 2004-2005.

(Air War Classics)

ISBN 1-903223-40-7. Vol. 1: Spartan to Normandy, June 1943 to June 1944

ISBN 1-903223-41-5. Vol. 2: Breakout to Bodenplatte, July 1944 to January 1945

SHORES, Christopher

Aces High: a Tribute to the Most Notable Fighter Pilots of the British and Commonwealth Forces in WWII by Christopher Shores and Clive Williams.

Rev. ed.; Grub Street, London, 1994.

ISBN 1-898697-00-0

SHORES, Christopher

Aces High: Vol 2: a Further Tribute to the Most Notable Fighter Pilots of the British and Commonwealth Air Forces in WWII by Christopher Shores.

Grub Street, London, 1998.

ISBN 1-9023-040-3-9

SHORES, Christopher

Air War for Burma: the Allied Air Forces Fight Back in South-East Asia, 1942-1945 by Christopher Shores.

Grub Street, London, 2005.

ISBN 1-904010-95-4

SHORES, Christopher
Air War for Yugoslavia, Greece and Crete 1940-41 by Christopher Shores and Brian Cull; with Nicola Malizia.
Grub Street, London, 1987.
ISBN 0-948817-07-0

SHORES, Christopher
Bloody Shambles. Volume One: the Drift to War to the Fall of Singapore by Christopher Shores and Brian Cull with Yasuho Izawa.
Grub Street, London, 1992.
ISBN 0-948817-50-X

SHORES, Christopher
Bloody Shambles. Volume 2: the Defence of Sumatra to the Fall of Burma by Christopher Shores and Brian Cull with Yasuho Izawa.
Grub Street, London, 1993.
ISBN 0-948817-67-4

SHORES, Christopher
Dust Clouds in the Middle East: the Air War for East Africa, Iraq, Syria, Iran and Madagascar, 1940-42 by Christopher Shores.
Grub Street, London, 1996.
ISBN 1-898697-37-X

SHORES, Christopher
Fighters over Tunisia by Christopher Shores, Hans Ring and William N Hess.
Neville Spearman, London, 1975.
ISBN 0-85435-210-4

SHORES, Christopher
Malta: the Spitfire Year 1942 by Christopher Shores and Brian Cull; with Nicola Malizia.
Grub Street, London, 1991.
ISBN 0-948817-16-X

SHORES, Christopher
Those Other Eagles: a Tribute to the British, Commonwealth and Free European Fighter Pilots Who Claimed Between Two and Four Victories in Aerial Combat 1939-1982: a Companion Volume to Aces High by Christopher Shores.
Grub Street, London, 2004.
ISBN 1-904010-88-1

TERRAINE, John
The Right of the Line: the Royal Air Force in the European War 1939-1945 by John Terraine.
Hodder and Stoughton, London, 1985.
ISBN 0-340-26644-9

WEBSTER, Charles
The Strategic Air Offensive against Germany 1939-1945: [4 volumes] by Sir Charles Webster and Noble Frankland.
HMSO, London, 1961.
(History of the Second World War; United Kingdom Military Series)

WILSON, Eunice
Dangerous Sky: a Resource Guide to the Battle of Britain by Eunice Wilson.
Greenwood Press, London, 1995.
(Bibliographies of Battles and Leaders; no. 14)
ISBN 0-313-28216-1

WOOD, Derek

The Narrow Margin: the Battle of Britain and the Rise of Air Power, 1930-1940 by Derek Wood; with Derek Dempster.

3rd ed.; Tri-Service Press, London, 1990.

ISBN 1-85488-027-6

POST 1945

FLINTHAM, Victor

Air Wars and Aircraft: a Detailed Record of Air Combat, 1945 to the Present by Victor Flintham.

Arms and Armour, London, 1989.

ISBN 0-85368-779-X

LEE, David

Eastward: a History of the Royal Air Force in the Far East, 1945-1972 by Air Chief Marshal Sir David Lee.

HMSO, London, 1984.

ISBN 0-11-772354-1

LEE, David

Flight from the Middle East: a History of the Royal Air Force in the Arabian Peninsula and Adjacent Territories, 1945-1972 by Air Chief Marshal Sir David Lee.

HMSO, London, 1980.

ISBN 0-11-772356-8

LEE, David

Wings in the Sun: a History of the Royal Air Force in the Mediterranean, 1945-1986 by Air Chief Marshal Sir David Lee CBE CB.

HMSO, London, 1989.

ISBN 0-11-772620-6

SQUADRONS AND UNITS

HALLEY, James J

The Squadrons of the Royal Air Force and Commonwealth, 1918-1988 by James J Halley.

Air-Britain (Historians), Tonbridge, Kent, 1988.

ISBN 0-85130-164-9

JEFFORD, CG

R.A.F. Squadrons: a Comprehensive Record of the Movement and Equipment of all RAF Squadrons and their Antecedents since 1912 by Wing Commander CG Jefford MBE, BA RAF (Retd.).

2nd ed.; Airlife, Shrewsbury, 2001.

ISBN 1-84037-141-2

MOYES, Philip JR

Bomber Squadrons of the R.A.F. and their Aircraft by Philip JR Moyes.

New ed.; Macdonald and Jane's, London, 1976.

RAWLINGS, John DR

Coastal, Support and Special Squadrons of the RAF and their Aircraft by John DR Rawlings.

Jane's, London, 1982.

ISBN 0-7106-0187-5

RAWLINGS, John DR

Fighter Squadrons of the R.A.F. and their Aircraft by John DR Rawlings.

Crecy, [Somerton], 1993.

ISBN 0-947554-24-6

STURTIVANT, Ray
Royal Air Force Flying Training and Support Units by Ray Sturtivant, John Hamlin and James J Halley.
Air Britain (Historians), Tunbridge Wells, Kent, 1997.
ISBN 0-85130-252-1

AIRFIELDS

ASHWORTH, Chris
Action Stations 5: Military Airfields of the South-West by Chris Ashworth.
2nd ed.; Patrick Stephens, Wellingborough, Northamptonshire, 1990.
ISBN 1-85260-374-7

ASHWORTH, Chris
Action Stations 9: Military Airfields of the Central South and South-East by Chris Ashworth.
Patrick Stephens, Wellingborough, Northamptonshire, 1986.
ISBN 0-85059-608-4

BOWYER, Michael JF
Action Stations 1: Wartime Military Airfields of East Anglia, 1939-1945 by Michael JF Bowyer.
Patrick Stephens, Cambridge, 1979.
ISBN 0-85059-335-2

BOWYER, Michael JF
Action Stations 6: Military Airfields of the Cotswolds and the Central Midlands by Michael JF Bowyer.
Patrick Stephens, Cambridge, 1983.
ISBN 0-85059-529-0

BOWYER, Michael JF
Action Stations Revisited: the Complete History of Britain's Military Airfields. No. 1: Eastern England by Michael JF Bowyer.
Crécy Publishing, Manchester, 2000.
ISBN 0-947554-79-3

BOWYER, Michael JF
Action Stations Revisited: Vol. 2: Central England and the London Area by Michael JF Bowyer.
Crécy Publishing, Manchester, 2003.
ISBN: 0-947554-94-7

FAIRBAIRN, Tony
Action Stations Overseas by Sqn Ldr Tony Fairbairn.
Patrick Stephens, Wellingborough, Northamptonshire, 1991.
ISBN 1-85260-319-4

FREEMAN, Roger A
Bases of Bomber Command: Then and Now by Roger A Freeman.
Battle of Britain International, London, 2001.
ISBN 1-870067-35-5

HALPENNY, Bruce Barrymore
Action Stations 2: Military Airfields of Lincolnshire and the East Midlands by Bruce Barrymore Halpenny.
2nd ed.; Patrick Stephens, n.p., 1991.
ISBN 1-85260-405-0

HALPENNY, Bruce Barrymore
Action Stations 4: Military Airfields of Yorkshire by Bruce Barrymore Halpenny.
Patrick Stephens, Cambridge, 1982.
ISBN 0-85059-532-0

HALPENNY, Bruce Barrymore
Action Stations 8: Military Airfields of Greater London by Bruce Barrymore Halpenny.
Patrick Stephens, Cambridge, 1984.
ISBN 0-85039-885-1

QUARRIE, Bruce
Action Stations 10: Supplement and Index compiled and edited by Bruce Quarrie.
Patrick Stephens, Wellingborough, Northamptonshire, 1987.
ISBN 0-85059-682-3

SMITH, David J
Action Stations 3: Military Airfields of Wales and the North West by David J Smith.
Patrick Stephens, Cambridge, 1981.
ISBN 0-85059-485-5

SMITH, David J
Action Stations 7: Military Airfields of Scotland, the North-East and Northern Ireland by David J Smith.
Patrick Stephens, Cambridge, 1983.
ISBN 0-85059-563-0

GENERAL

ADKIN, FRED
Through the Hangar Doors by Fred Adkin.
Airlife, Shrewsbury, 1986.
ISBN 0-906393-59-0

BEAUMAN, Katharine Bentley
Partners in Blue: the Story of Women's Service with the Royal Air Force by Katharine Bentley Beauman.
Hutchinson, London, 1971.
ISBN 0-09-105860-0

CONGDON, Philip
Per Ardua Ad Astra: a Handbook of the Royal Air Force by Philip Congdon.
2nd ed.; Airlife, Shrewsbury, 1994.
ISBN 1-85310-478-7

DELVE, Ken
The Source Book of the RAF by Ken Delve.
Airlife Publishing, Shrewsbury, 1994.
ISBN 1-85310-451-1

ESCOTT, Beryl E
Women in Air Force Blue: the Story of Women in the Royal Air Force from 1918 to the Present Day by Squadron Leader Beryl E Escott.
Patrick Stephens, Cambridge, 1989.
ISBN 1-85260-066-7

FERTE, Philip Joubert de la
The Forgotten Ones: the Story of the Ground Crews by Air Chief Marshal Sir Philip Joubert de la Ferté, KCB, CMG, DSO.
Hutchinson, London, 1961.

JEFFORD, CG
Observers and Navigators and Other Non-Pilot Aircrew in the RFC, RNAS and RAF by Wing Commander CG Jefford MBE, BA, RAF Retd.
Airlife, Shrewsbury, 2001.
ISBN 1-84037-275-3

MACKIE, Mary

Sky Wards: a History of the Princess Mary's Royal Air Force Nursing Service by Mary Mackie; foreword by HRH The Princess Alexandra Patron of the PMRAFNS.

Robert Hale, London, 2001.

ISBN 0-7090-6976-6

OLIVER, Kingsley M

Through Adversity: the History of the Royal Air Force Regiment, 1942-1992 by Kingsley M Oliver.

Forces and Corporate Publishing, Rushden, Northamptonshire, 1997.

ISBN 0-9529597-0-4

WYNN, Humphrey

Forged in War: a History of RAF Transport Command by Humphrey Wynn.

HMSO, London, 1996.

ISBN 0-11-772756-3

MEDALS AND AWARDS

CAMPAIGN MEDALS

DYMOND, Steve

Researching British Military Medals: a Practical Guide by Steve Dymond.

Crowood Press, Marlborough, Wiltshire, 1999.

ISBN 1-86126-282-5

GOULD, Robert W

British Campaign Medals: Waterloo to the Gulf by Robert W Gould.

4th rev. ed.; Arms and Armour, London, 1994.

ISBN 1-85409-224-3

JOSLIN, EC

British Battles and Medals by EC Joslin, AR Litherland and BT Simpkin.
6th ed.; Spink, London, 1988.
ISBN 0-907605-25-7

WILLIAMSON, HJ

Collecting and Researching the Campaign Medals of the Great War by HJ Williamson.
Harwich Printing Co, Harwich, Essex, 1989

GALLANTRY AWARDS

Naval and Air Force Honours and Awards...
Hayward and Son, London, n.d.
ISBN 0-903754-07-X
[facsimile reproduction of information originally published in the *Navy List* of April 1919 and the *Air Force List* of April 1920]

The Register of the George Cross.
This England Books, Cheltenham, 1985.
ISBN 0-906324-06-8

The Register of the Victoria Cross.
Rev. ed.; This England Books, Cheltenham, 1988.
ISBN 0-906324-07-6

ABBOTT, PE

British Gallantry Awards by PE Abbott and JMA Tamplin.
Nimrod Dix, London, 1981.

AUSTERBERRY, Bernard Ronald
Gazetted Awards to NCOs and Other Ranks of the Aerial Forces, 1914-1924 compiled by Bernard Ronald Austerberry
Jade Publishing, Uppermill, Oldham, Lancashire, 1999.
ISBN 0-9518098-6-5

CARTER, Nick and Carol
The Distinguished Flying Cross and How it was Won, 1918-1995 by Nick and Carol Carter.
Savannah Publications, n.p., 1998.
ISBN 1-902366-00-X

COOPER, Alan W
In Action with the Enemy: the Holders of the Conspicuous Gallantry Medal (Flying) by Alan W Cooper.
William Kimber, London, 1986.
ISBN 0-7183-0621-X

CREAGH, O'Moore
The VC and DSO: a Complete Record of all those Officers, Non-Commissioned Officers and Men of His Majesty's Naval, Military and Air Forces who have been Awarded these Decorations from the Time of their Institution...: [3 volumes] edited by the late Sir O'Moore Creagh (until 1920) and EM Humphris; with a foreword by Earl Beatty, Earl of Cavan and Sir HM Trenchard.
Standard Art Book, London, [1924].

HENDERSON, DV
Dragons can be Defeated: a Complete Record of the George Medal's Progress, 1940-1983 compiled by DV Henderson.
Spink and Son, London, 1984.
ISBN 0-90-7605-14-1

NELSON, Kenneth James

The Royal Air Force Awards 1918-1919: being the Distinguished Flying Cross, Air Force Cross, Distinguished Flying Medal, Air Force Medal compiled by Kenneth James Nelson.
KJ Nelson, N.p., 2000.
ISBN 0-9698625-1-2

TAVENDER, IT

The Distinguished Flying Medal: a Record of Courage, 1918-1982 by IT Tavender.
JB Hayward, Polstead, Suffolk, 1990.
ISBN 0-903754-43-6

TAVENDER, IT

The Distinguished Flying Medal Register for the Second World War: with Official Recommendation Details [2 volumes Volume 1: A-J; Volume 2: K-Z] by Ian Tavender.
Savannah, London: 2000.
ISBN 1-902366-03-4

CASUALTIES, ROLLS OF HONOUR AND MEMORIALS

The National Roll of the Great War 1914-1918. Sections I-XV.
National Publishing, London, [1920-1922?].
[complete set held by IWM – includes recently compiled index volume]

BEATY, David

Light Perpetual: Aviators' Memorial Windows by David Beaty.
Airlife, Shrewsbury, 1995.
ISBN 1-85310-588-0

CAMPBELL, GL
Royal Flying Corps 'Per Ardua Ad Astra': (Military Wing): Casualties and Honours during the War of 1914-17 compiled by Captain GL Campbell; assisted by RH Blinkhorn.
Picture Advertising Company, London, 1917.

CHORLEY, WR
Royal Air Force Bomber Command Losses of the Second World War: [8 volumes] by WR Chorley.
Midland Counties Publications, Leicester, 1992-2003.
ISBN 0-904597-85-X. Volume 1: Aircraft and Crew Losses during 1939-1940
ISBN 0-904597-87-3. Volume 2: Aircraft and Crew Losses, 1941
ISBN 0-904597-89-X. Volume 3: Aircraft and Crew Losses, 1942
ISBN 0-904597-90-3. Volume 4: Aircraft and Crew Losses, 1943
ISBN 0-904597-91-1. Volume 5: Aircraft and Crew Losses, 1944
ISBN 0-904597-92-X. Volume 6: Aircraft and Crew Losses, 1945
ISBN 1-85780-132-6. Volume 7: Operational Training Units 1940-1947
ISBN 1 85780-156-3. Volume 8: Heavy Conversion Units and Miscellaneous Units, 1939-1947

CUMMINGS, Colin
Final Landings: a Summary of RAF Aircraft and Combat Losses, 1946 to 1949 compiled and edited by Colin Cummings.
Nimbus Publishing, Yelvertoft, Northamptonshire, [2004?].
ISBN 0-9526619-4-2

CUMMINGS, Colin
Last Take-Off: a Record of RAF Aircraft Losses, 1950 to 1953 compiled and edited by Colin Cummings.
Nimbus Publishing, Yelvertoft, Northamptonshire, [2004?].
ISBN 0-9526619-3-4

CUMMINGS, Colin

Lost to Service: a Summary of Accidents to RAF Aircraft and Losses of Personnel, 1959 to 1996 compiled and edited by Colin Cummings.

Nimbus Publishing, Yelvertoft, Northamptonshire, [1999?].

ISBN 0-9526619-0-X

CUMMINGS, Colin

To Fly No More: RAF Aircraft Accidents and Write-Offs, 1954-1958 compiled and edited by Colin Cummings.

Nimbus Publishing, Yelvertoft, Northamptonshire, [2004?].

ISBN 0-9526619-2-6

DONNELLY, Larry

The Other Few: Bomber and Coastal Command Operations in the Battle of Britain by Larry Donnelly.

Red Kite, Walton on Thames, Surrey, 2004.

ISBN 0-9546201-2-7

FRANKS, Norman LR

Royal Air Force Fighter Command Losses of the Second World War: Operational Losses: Aircraft and Crews, 1939-1945: [3 volumes] / Norman LR Franks.

Midland Publishing, Leicester, 1997-2000.

ISBN 1-85780-055-9 (pbk.). Volume 1 : 1939-1941

ISBN 1-85780-075-3 (pbk.). Volume 2 : 1942-1943

ISBN 1-85780-093-1 (pbk.). Volume 3 : Air Defence Great Britain, 2nd Tactical AirForce, and Fighter Command : 1944-1945

HENSHAW, Trevor
The Sky their Battlefield: Air Fighting and the Complete List of Allied Air Casualties from Enemy Action in the First War: British, Commonwealth, and United States Air Services 1914 to 1918 by Trevor Henshaw.
Grub Street, London, 1995.
ISBN 0-898697-30-2

HOBSON, Chris
Airmen Died in the Great War 1914-1918: the Roll of Honour of the British and Commonwealth Air Services of the First World War compiled by Chris Hobson.
JB Hayward and Son, Suffolk, 1995.
ISBN 0-871505-81-X

JARVIS, SD
Cross of Sacrifice. Volume 1: Officers who Died in the Service of British, Indian and East African Regiments and Corps 1914-1919 by SD and DB Jarvis.
Roberts Medals, Reading, 1993.
ISBN 1-873058-26-8

JARVIS, SD
Cross of Sacrifice. Volume 2: Officers who Died in the Service of the Royal Navy, Royal Naval Reserve, Royal Naval Volunteer Reserve, Royal Marines, Royal Naval Air Service and Royal Air Force, 1914-1919 by SD and DB Jarvis.
Roberts, Reading, 1993.
ISBN 1-873058-31-4

JARVIS, SD
Cross of Sacrifice. Volume 4: Non-Commissioned Officers, Men and Women of the United Kingdom, Commonwealth and Empire who Died in the Service of the Royal Navy, Royal Marines, Royal Naval Air Service, Royal Air Force, 1914-1921: including the Commonwealth Navies and Air Forces by SD and DB Jarvis.
Roberts, Reading, 1996.
ISBN 1-873058-41-1

MACPHERSON, WG

Medical Services. General History [4 vols] by Major-General Sir WG Macpherson.

HMSO, London, 1921-1924.

(History of the Great War based on Official Documents)

MCINNES, I

A Contemptible Little Flying Corps: being a Definitive and Previously Non-existent Roll of those Warrant Officers, NCO's and Airmen who Served in the Royal Flying Corps Prior to the Outbreak of the First World War by I McInnes and JV Webb.

London Stamp Exchange, London, 1991.

ISBN 0-948130-98-9

MCNEILL, Ross

Royal Air Force Coastal Command Losses of the Second World War by Ross McNeill.

Midland Publishing, Hinckley, Leicestershire, 2003.

ISBN 1-85780-128-8 (pbk.). Vol. 1: Aircraft and Crew Losses 1939-1941

NORMAN, Bill

Failed to Return: the Yorkshire Memorials to the Bomber Squadrons of No 4 Group RAF and No 6 (RCAF) Group, 1939-1945 by Bill Norman.

Leo Cooper, London, 1995.

ISBN 0-85052-474-1

REXFORD-WELCH, SC

The Royal Air Force Medical Services [3 vols] edited by Squadron Leader SC Rexford-Welch.

HMSO, London, 1954-1958.

(History of the Second World War. United Kingdom Medical Series)

SMITH, David J

Britain's Aviation Memorials and Mementoes by David J Smith.
Patrick Stephens, Yeovil, Somerset, 1992.
ISBN 1-85260-395-X

WILLIAMSON, HJ

The Roll of Honour, Royal Flying Corps and Royal Air Force for the Great War, 1914-1918 by HJ Williamson.
Naval and Military Press, Dallington, Sussex, 1992.
ISBN 1-879632-20-7

WYNN, Kenneth G

Men of the Battle of Britain: a Biographical Directory of 'the Few' by Kenneth G Wynn.
2nd ed.; CCB Associates, South Croydon, 1999.

PRISONERS OF WAR

List of British Officers Taken Prisoner in the Various Theatres of War between August 1914 and November 1918 compiled from records kept by Messrs Cox and Co's Enquiry Office.
Cox, London, 1919.

Prisoners of War: Naval and Air Forces of Great Britain and the Empire, 1939-1945: Alphabetical Nominal Registers (Including Number, Rank/Rating, POW Number and Camp Location Details) Listing Over 21,000 Australian, British, Canadian, New Zealand, South African and Other Naval and Air Force Prisoners of War of All Ranks Held in Germany and German Occupied Territories...(All Lists Corrected Generally Up To 30th March 1945).
JB Hayward in association with the Imperial War Museum, Department of Printed Books, Polstead, Suffolk, 1990.
ISBN 0-903754-62-2

CLUTTON-BROCK, Oliver

Footprints on the Sands of Time: RAF Bomber Command Prisoners-of-War in Germany, 1939-1945 by Oliver Clutton-Brock.

Grub Street, London, 2003.

ISBN 1-904010-35-0

GAMMON, Victor F

No Time for Fear: True Accounts of RAF Airmen taken Prisoner, 1939-1945 by Victor F Gammon.

Arms and Armour, London, 1998.

ISBN 1-85409-490-4

GAMMON, Victor F

Not All Glory!: True Accounts of RAF Airmen taken Prisoner in Europe, 1939-1945 by Victor F Gammon.

Arms and Armour, London, 1996.

ISBN 1-85409-337-1

MASON, W Wynne

Prisoners of War by W Wynne Mason.

War History Branch, Department of Internal Affairs, Wellington, New Zealand, 1954.

(Official History of New Zealand in the Second World War, 1939-45)

NICHOL, John

The Last Escape: the Untold Story of Allied Prisoners of War in Germany, 1944-45 by John Nichol and Tony Rennell.

Viking, London, 2002.

ISBN 0-670-91094-5

POPE-HENNESSY, Mrs

Map of the Main Prison Camps in Germany and Austria by Mrs Pope-Hennessy.

Nisbet, London, [191-?]

[facsimile reprint available from the Department of Printed Books]

ROLF, David
Prisoners of the Reich: Germany's Captives, 1939-1945 by David Rolf.
Leo Cooper, London, 1988.
ISBN 0-85052-681-7

ROLLINGS, Charles
Wire and Walls: RAF Prisoners of War in Itzehoe, Spangenberg and Thorn, 1939-42 by Charles Rollings.
Ian Allan Publishing, Hersham, Surrey, 2003.
ISBN 0-7110-2991-1

ROLLINGS, Charles
Wire and Worse: RAF Prisoners of War in Laufen, Biberach, Lübeck and Warburg, 1940-42 by Charles Rollings.
Ian Allan Publishing, Hersham, Surrey, 2004.
ISBN 0-7110-3050-2

STUBBS, Les
Unsung Heroes of the Royal Air Force: the Far East Prisoners of War, 1941-1945 by Les and Pam Stubbs.
Barry Books, Grantham, Lincolnshire, 2002.
ISBN 1-903172-21-7

WATERFORD, Van
Prisoners of the Japanese in World War II: Statistical History, Personal Narratives, and Memorials concerning POWs in Camps and on Hellships, Civilian Internees, Asian Slave Laborers and Others Captured in the Pacific Theater by Van Waterford.
McFarland, Jefferson, North Carolina, 1994.
ISBN 0-89950-893-6

RESEARCH FACILITIES AT THE IMPERIAL WAR MUSEUM

THE READING ROOM

Formerly the chapel of the Bethlem Royal Hospital, or Bedlam, this historic room is used extensively by authors, scholars, journalists, broadcasters and visitors alike. Readers have access to a major reference library of printed materials encompassing everything from trench maps to a vast journals collection. The Department of Documents holds an extensive collection of unpublished diaries, letters and memoirs of servicemen and women and civilians.

Access to the Reading Room is free but you should make an appointment in advance.

Monday – Saturday 10.00am-5.00pm
Closed: Bank Holiday weekends, 24, 25, 26 December and for a period of 2 weeks (usually May) for stocktaking purposes

When making an appointment please give us as much detail of your area of research as possible. Material can then be pre-selected and ready on your arrival. However, this should not deter you from a further catalogue search of your own. We will be happy to show you the various catalogues and options open to you. Bags are not generally allowed in the reading room – these should be left in the cloakroom – although handbags and portable computers are admissible. Please remember that this is an old building and, although we have done much to improve the provision of electric points, lighting and ventilation, we are limited by the amount of physical space actually available. We will, however, always try to accommodate anyone wishing to consult our collections. The design limitations of this building make access to the Reading Room difficult for many disabled visitors but alternative facilities are available. Please ask when making your appointment.

Photocopying and other services

Guidance on photocopying procedures is available in printed form in the Reading Room itself. We are bound by the copyright law, and by our own conservation and preservation requirements. Black and white photocopies are available at a fixed Museum price and special photography can be arranged. Booklists and information sheets are available on a variety of subjects.

Our contact details:

Department of Printed Books
Imperial War Museum, Lambeth Road, London SE1 6HZ
Tel: 020 7416 5342 (for general enquiries and appointments)
Fax: 020 7416 5246
E-mail: books@iwm.org.uk

Department of Documents
Imperial War Museum, Lambeth Road, London SE1 6HZ
Tel: 020 7416 5222
Fax: 020 7416 5374
E-mail: docs@iwm.org.uk

Other Collecting Departments
[all postal enquiries should be addressed to the appropriate department at Imperial War Museum, Lambeth Road, London SE1 6HZ]

Department of Art
Material may be seen by prior appointment in the Print Room at the Museum's Lambeth Road branch, Tuesday-Thursday, 10.00am-5.00pm. To arrange a visit, contact the Department's Research and Information Officer.
Tel: 020 7416 5211
E-mail: art@iwm.org.uk

Department of Exhibits and Firearms
A visitor's room is open by appointment, Monday-Friday, 10.00am-5.00pm.
Tel: 020 7416 5308
Fax: 020 7416 5374
E-mail: exfire@iwm.org.uk

Film and Photograph Archives

The Film Archive is open by appointment from Monday-Friday, 10.00am-5.00pm. At least 24 hours notice is normally sufficient to research the catalogue, but 5-7 days notice is required to view any film selected. Film viewing and handling fees are charged. The Visitor's Room is located at: All Saints Annexe, Austral Street, London SE11.
Tel: 020 7416 5291 / 5292
Fax: 020 7416 5299
E-mail: film@iwm.org.uk

The Photograph Archive Visitors' Room at the All Saints Annexe, Austral Street, is open to visitors, by appointment, from Monday-Friday, 10.00am-5.00pm.
Tel: 020 7416 5333 / 5338 [Please allow a minimum of 24 hours notice]
Fax: 020 7416 5355
E-mail: photos@iwm.org.uk

Sound Archive

The Visitors Room at the All Saints Annexe, Austral Street is open by appointment, Monday to Friday, 10.00am-5.00pm. Visitors may listen to tapes and consult printed and database catalogues; some typescripts available.
Tel: 020 7416 5363
E-mail: sound@iwm.org.uk

Collections Online

An exciting new development has been the launch of **Collections Online** at **www.iwmcollections.org.uk**
The initial tranche of material was made public in 2002, and catalogues from all the Collecting Departments were made

available in 2004. For the first time you can access the Museum's catalogues online. If you want to browse there are short essays on major historical themes, which lead you to selected highlights from all over the collections, including artworks, documents, exhibits, film, photographs and sound recordings. Currently 160,000 records are available, although it is important to realise that no catalogue is ever totally complete – if you don't find what you are looking for, please contact us and ask.

GENERAL CONTACTS

The Museum has five branches. These are:

Imperial War Museum London
Lambeth Road, London SE1 6HZ
Open daily, 10.00am-6.00pm
Tel: 020 7416 5320 / 5321 (general enquiries)
Fax: 020 7416 5374
E-mail: mail@iwm.org.uk

Churchill Museum and Cabinet War Rooms
Clive Steps, King Charles Street, London SW1A 2AQ
Open daily
Summer (1 April-30 September) 9.30am-6.00pm
last admission 5.15pm
Winter 10.00am-6.00pm, last admission 5.15pm
Tel: 020 7930 6961
Fax: 020 7839 5897
E-mail: cwr@iwm.org.uk

HMS *Belfast*
Morgan's Lane, Tooley Street, London SE1 2JH
Open daily
Summer (1 March-31 October) 10.00am-6.00pm, last admission 5.15pm
Winter 10.00am-5.00pm, last admission 4.15pm
Tel: 020 7940 6300
Fax: 020 7403 0719
E-mail: hmsbelfast@iwm.org.uk

Imperial War Museum Duxford
Cambridgeshire CB2 4QR
Open daily
Summer (mid March-mid October) 10.00am-6.00pm, last admission 5.15pm
Winter 10.00am-4.00pm, last admission 3.15pm
Tel: 01223 835000
Fax: 01223 837267
E-mail: duxford@iwm.org.uk

Imperial War Museum North
The Quays, Trafford Wharf, Trafford Park, Manchester M17 1TZ
Open daily
Summer (1 March-31 October) 10.00am-6.00pm, last admission 5.30pm
Winter 10.00am-5.00pm, last admission 4.30pm
Tel: 0161 836 4000
Fax: 0161 836 4012
E-mail: iwmnorth@iwm.org.uk

All branches are closed 24, 25, 26 December

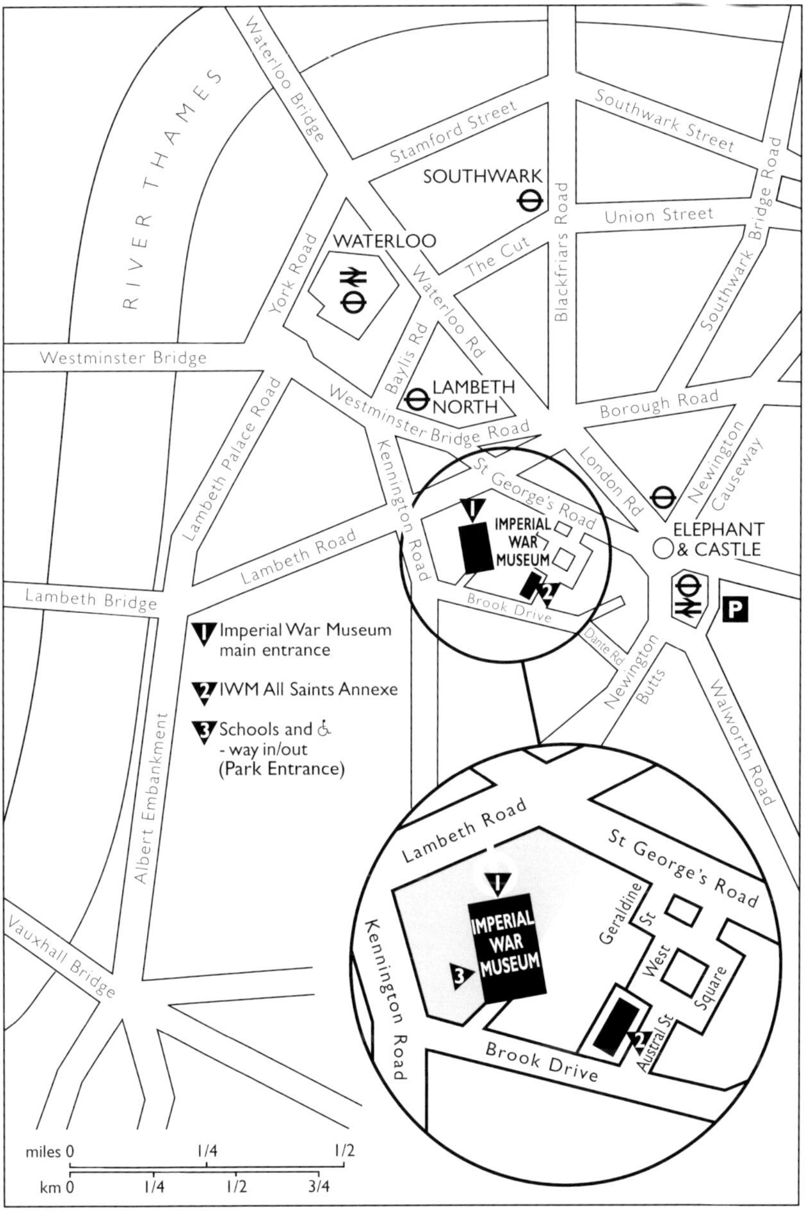

www.iwm.org.uk